Gatherings

&

Traditions

This Cookbook Belongs To:

**A cookbook by the
Service League of Cherokee County
Canton, Georgia**

Proceeds from the sales of *Gatherings & Traditions* will be used to provide food, clothing, school supplies, medical assistance and scholarships to families and children in need.

First Printing – 2013

To order additional copies of

Gatherings & Traditions

Please visit us at our website www.serviceleague.net or use the forms provided in the back of the book.

Library of Congress Card Number

ISBN: 978-1-935397-69-4

Printed in the U.S.A. by
Fundcraft Publishing
P.O. Box 340, Collierville, TN 38027
800-853-1363 www.fundcraft.com

The Cookbook Committee wishes to thank the League members, Honorary Members, family and friends who so graciously shared their special recipes. We appreciate the time, hard work, dedication, and most importantly, the passion for this special project each of you contributed. This was truly a labor of love for what the League represents to the community we work so hard to be of service to. To our families, a very special thank you for your patience and support during the past two years. It has been an honor to work on this project.

Cookbook Committee

Lisa Woodruff – Co-Chairman
Bonny Spears – Co-Chairman
Lori Davis – Co-Vice-Chairman
Julie Pennington – Co-Vice-Chairman

2012-14 Committee

Melissa Auringer
Kim Barger
Jade Bergdoll
Heather Cato
Kim Fowler
Meghan Griffin
Barbara Jacoby

Patti Martin
Robyn McEntyre
Ashley Rushbridge
Jodi Sears
Delane Stevens
April Turner

2011-2012 Committee

Melissa Auringer
Jade Bergdoll
Allison Higgins
Barbara Jacoby
Amy Kelley
Patti Martin

Molly Mercer
Jodi Sears
Erin Thomas
April Turner
Joanne Waver

Service League of Cherokee County
2013 - 2014 Members

Deanna Adkins
Jana Anderman
Jennifer Arp
Melissa Auringer
Stephanie Bagwell
Stacy Benson
Kim Barger
Tammy Beasley
Shiela Benz
Jade Bergdoll
Michelle Bowden
Leslie Bowers
Kelly Brannam
Anne Burke
Shannan Cagle
Nicole Carnes
Heather Cato
Renee Cavan
Millie Cline
Jennifer Connelly
Beth Cornelison
Bianca Cummings
Lori Davis
Paula Evans
Kimberly Fowler
Katie Garrison
Kristin Gauthier
Amy Graham
Betsy Graham
Meghan Griffin
Hillary Hall

Angie Hathcock
Brittany Hayes
Alison Hendrix
Alison Higgins
Deidre Hollands
Jenny Hopkins
Amy Howell
Kelley Hyde
Susan Ikerd
Barbara Jacoby
Emily Jobe
Nellie Johnson
Taylor Johnson
Lori Karnes
Amy Kelley
Holli Kimsey
JoAnne Knieriem
Wendy Landry
Terry Lee
Julie Little
Amanda Locke
Beth Major
Patti Martin
Robyn McEntyre
Shelley McNellie
Molly Mercer
Gina Mickler
Gini Mizelle
Kristen Morris
Jaimee Moss
Brandy Murphy

Julie Pennington
Julie Peppers
Cindy Prien
Charlee Renfro
Tracy Roach
Courtney Robertson
Melissa Roper
Stacye Rubelsky
Ashley Rusbridge
Jodi Sears
Natalie Smith
Bonny Spears
Liz Spell
Jennifer Stanley
Laura Stanley
Emilie Steele
Delane Stevens
Marcy Stogner
Lynn Struck
Erin Thomas
April Turner
Elizabeth Wall
Amy Wallace
Sherry Wallace
Beth Watkins
Michele Webb
Melissa Whatley
Angela Wilson
Lisa Woodruff

Honorary League Members

Sara Jones*
Helen Vandiviere*
Sue Garlington*
Mary Darnell*
Nina Jones*
Eva Foster*
Evelena Haworth*
Bill Daniel*
Marie Pressly*
Grace Hyatt*
Betty Coker-Patrick*
Peggy Jones*
Mary Jones*
Hattie Mae Price*
Martha Fincher*
Marjorie McCanless*
Sally Boring*
Elizabeth Garrett*
Lynn Jones*
Frances Owen*
Clarice Bagwell*
Elizabeth Andrews*
Selene Hendrix*
Thelma "Tissie"
   Jones*
Ann Fincher
Virginia Jones*
Patricia Alexander*
Ann Cullens*
Rachel Palmer*
Virginia Spears
Martha Jane Haney*
Mrs. H.L. Buffington,
   Jr.*
Ruth Denney*
Mary Sparks*
Lane Towers*
Lillian Thomason*

Sara Lathem
Frances Pulliam*
Beth Raines*
Ann Weeks
Ann Bradshaw
Charlotte Gray*
Sybil Turner
Peggy Moore
Betty Barrett
Hazel Price
Elaine Swift*
Carolyn Vancil*
Dot Anderson
Martha Brigham
Barbara Manous
Eugenia Reid*
Sue Ellen Turner*
Ann Rutledge
Ann Hopkins
Pat Stewart
Jo Ellen Wilson
Raye Snell
Ann Fincher
Barbara Helton
Mary Johnston
Joan McFather
Linda Merrell
Barbara Gentry
Patti Mann
Linda Schwamlein
Peggy Rutledge
Margaret Logan
Joan Anderson
Shirley Pahl
Helen Spears
Cissy Cloud
Linda Hasty
Jeannie Adams*

Deborah Fincher
Wanda Roach
Frances Gober
Judy McGarity
Susan Padgett-
   Harrison
Julia Dennis
Carole Haley
Lila Stevens
Judy Bishop
Deanie Fincher
Pat Gold
Debra Goodwin
Rebecca Johnston
Mandy Mills
Ann Benzel
Christi Hinkley
Madelin Gray
Anne Harris
Joy Owen
Carolyn Weaver
Paula DeLuca
Marlene Hefner
Lynn Payne
Ollie White
Kathy Yarbrough*
Linda Bell
Cathy Conway
Christie Geiger
Carla Roach
Paula Holtzclaw
Alicia McComb
Dianne Murphy
Sally Bradshaw
Debbie Haygood
Lynda McFarland

* Deceased

E

Honorary League Members

Susan Dreschel
Kay Halpin
Rena Weatherby
Joan Lumpkin
Charlotte Sparks
Michelle Whitmire
Pam Chandler
Janie Cuzzort
Joan Duff
Kim Groves
Karen Hawley
Jamie Morgan
Veda Moss
Susan Thacker
Pam Carnes
Paula Doss
Kebra Galt
Connie Garrison
Lynn Satterfield
Patti Skelton
Tracy Weaver
Candy Wilbanks
Teresa Foster
Vicki Smith
Michelle Thacker
Mary Wuestefeld
Beth Allison
Leslie Campbell
Judy Christopher
Letitia Cline
Sandy Simmons
Dana Swords
Dawn Wilbanks
Becky Buice
Sandra Garcia
Karen McClellan
Kaye Rogers
Dee Walker

Beth Boyette
Jenny Brooks
Kathy Hulsey
Angela Norton
Julie Rogers
Carolyn Stevens
Angie Whitaker
Cheryl Young
Anita Geoghagan
Pam Grant
Beth Johnston
Andrea Payne
Michelle Prance
Maggie Reneau
Chrissy Snelson
Jenny Thacker
Kim Thompson
Lori Bagwell
Mandy Bobo
Kelly Cline
Susie Everett
Terri Harris
Catherine Holman
Valerie Lowery
Kipling Mann
Rhonda Patterson
Kelly Underwood
Mia Temples
Neda Chester
Stacy Parker
Janet Wheeler
Julie White
Carla Barnes
Jamie Bobo
Beth Brandon
Anna Hasty
Suzanne Holloway
Emily Reinhart

Holly Ricketts
Stacy Yawn
Amy Blanton
Laurie Carroll
Brandy Looper
Janet Roach
Terry Sams
Joanne Waver
Jory Cannon
Denise Cooper
Judy Key
Debbie Murdock

* Deceased

TABLE OF CONTENTS

appetizers

Relishes
& pickles

Appetizers

Appetizers are treats that can be served either at the start of a meal or at a reception or open house. Listed below are suggestions for quick and easy appetizers, along with some advice to follow for staying within the guidelines for a healthy diet:

Salsa has become one of America's most popular foods, primarily from its abundant use as an appetizer. Not only is salsa tasty, but it contains little or no fat.

For a change from basic salsa, mix with an equal amount of refried beans and top with cheese. Heat in the microwave and serve hot.

Chips are the natural companion to salsa, including potato chips and corn chips. Most potato and corn chips are fried, and therefore, contain a high level of fat. Baked chips, or even baked pretzels, are a good alternative when used with salsa. The taste of the salsa generally makes up for any loss of taste from baked rather than fried chips.

Cut, raw vegetables arranged on a tray can make a decorative and colorful appetizer. Salad dressings make easy vegetable dips, but try to use low-fat versions. Most regular salad dressings are loaded with fat. Low-fat sour cream can be mixed with ketchup and garlic powder to make an easy vegetable dip.

Cream cheese has long been a versatile food to build a quick appetizer around. Reduced fat cream cheeses are a good choice. Top cream cheese with any of the following for a quick and easy appetizer:

- green pepper jelly
- drained small shrimp and cocktail sauce
- chopped pickle or pickle relish
- a dash of worcestershire sauce and chives
- chopped chutney and a dash of curry powder

Each of these combinations can be served with crackers, thin-sliced toast or chips.

APPETIZERS, RELISHES & PICKLES

PPLE DIP

1 tub Marzetti's caramel dip
8 oz. cream cheese, softened

1 pkg. Heath bar bits

In a large bowl, mix together a generous scoop of caramel dip and softened cream cheese. Spread in a pie plate. Top with remaining caramel. Follow with a solid layer of Heath bits. Serve with apples.

Laura Stanley

APPLE HEATH BAR DIP

¾ c. brown sugar
½ c. sugar
1 tsp. vanilla
1 c. Heath bar

8 oz. cream cheese
1 large can pineapple juice
8 Granny Smith green apples

Slice the apples and let them soak in the pineapple juice to prevent them turning brown. After they have soaked for 20 minutes or so, drain the pineapple juice and place on the dish you want to serve them on.

Mix the other ingredients and place in the refrigerator for at least 30 minutes to an hour.

Kim Fowler

BACON WRAPS

1 pkg. Little Smokies
1 lb. bacon

1 small bag brown sugar

You will need toothpicks.

Cut bacon into thirds. Wrap a small piece of bacon around each Smokie. Use a toothpick to secure the bacon. Place in a 9 x 13 baking dish. Cover the Smokies with brown sugar. Bake at 350° for 30 minutes or until bacon is at your desired crispness.

Amy Graham

ℬUFFALO CHICKEN DIP

2 (10 oz.) cans chicken, drained
1 c. mild Cheddar cheese, shredded
1 (8 oz.) block cream cheese
1 c. Ranch or Bleu cheese dressing
¾ c. Frank's or Pete's hot sauce

Preheat oven to 350°. Mix cream cheese, Ranch dressing and hot sauce in a saucepan over low heat. Chop up the chicken so there are no big chunks. Add the chicken. Mix together until cream cheese is melted and the chicken is mixed well into the dressing and hot sauce. Turn off the heat, add the Cheddar cheese and mix together until the cheese is melted. Pour into a baking dish and bake 20 minutes at 350°. Serve with crackers or tortilla chips.

Spiciness can be adjusted by adding a hotter style sauce or a milder one, depending on your taste. Can be made the night before and refrigerated until ready to serve. Baking time will take longer if the mixture has just come out of the refrigerator.

Lori Davis

𝒞HEDDAR CRACKERS

8 oz. sharp Cheddar, finely grated (I use food processor)
2 sticks softened butter
6 dashes of Tabasco sauce
½ tsp. salt
1 tsp. dried herbs (dill, thyme, rosemary, Italian, cayenne; anything will work)
2 c. all-purpose flour

Combine the cheese and the butter and the Tabasco. Mix the flour and herbs and salt together. Add it to the butter and cheese in thirds and beat it thoroughly each time. Divide your dough into 4 reasonably equal portions and shape into logs 1 ½-inches in diameter. Wrap in Saran Wrap and refrigerate for 2 hours or until firm.

Preheat the oven to 325° and spray the cookie sheets. Slice logs about ¼-inch thick and put on sheet. These don't spread much, so you can get bunches on each sheet. Bake about 15 minutes; the centers might look a little soft, but they will firm up. These will go from golden brown to burnt in a nanosecond, so watch them! This recipe will make 6 dozen. This is double the original recipe already, because what good are only 3 dozen of these?

Wanda Roach
Honorary Member

CHEESE BALL

1 (12.5 oz.) can chicken
1 envelope Hidden Valley
   Original Ranch mix

1 (8 oz.) whipped cream
   cheese
chopped pecans

Mix the first 3 ingredients together. Use wax paper to form the mixture into a ball. Place a circle of chopped pecans on a piece of plastic wrap and transfer the cheese ball onto the pecans. Pat remaining pecans over the rest of the cheese ball. Wrap cheese ball in the plastic wrap and further shape into a ball. Refrigerate for several hours or overnight. Serve with mini Club crackers.

Millie Cline

CHEESE STRAWS

1 lb. Cracker Barrel cheese
   (8 oz. sharp, 8 oz. mild)
2 sticks margarine
2 ½ c. plain flour
1 tsp. salt

¼ tsp. red pepper (cayenne)
dash of Tabasco sauce
1 tsp. garlic (more or less to
   taste)

Grate cheese. Add other ingredients. Mix thoroughly. Roll onto slightly floured board. Cut with pizza cutter in desired length. Bake on greased cookie sheet until brown at 375°.

Amy Howell

CHEESE TRUFFLES

1 container (8 oz.) cream
   cheese spread
1 garlic clove, pressed
¼ tsp. Tabasco hot pepper
   sauce (optional)

1 pkg. (8 oz.) finely shredded
   Cheddar cheese
½ c. coarsely chopped
   almonds, pecans or snipped
   fresh parsley

In large bowl, combine cream cheese spread, garlic and pepper sauce, if desired; mix well. Add Cheddar cheese in cream cheese mixture (mixture will be stiff). Using a small cookie scoop, drop level scoops of cheese mixture onto cutting board. Coat cheese balls in chopped almonds, pecans or parsley. Serve using toothpicks or with assorted crackers, if desired.

Bonny Spears

*C*HILI CHEESE PINWHEELS

8 oz. cream cheese
2 c. shredded Cheddar cheese
1 (4 oz.) can diced green
   chilies

6 green onions, diced
1 c. chopped red bell pepper
1 can black olives, chopped
6 to 8 large flour tortillas

Combine cream cheese, Cheddar cheese, chilies, green onions, bell peppers and olives in medium bowl. Spread ½ cup cheese mixture over each tortilla or until desired thickness; roll up. Wrap each roll in plastic wrap and refrigerate for 2 hours. Remove plastic wrap, slice each roll into 2-inch pieces and serve.

For a better tasting pinwheel, refrigerate wraps overnight before slicing. Ingredients blend better over time.

Lori Davis

*C*OLD CHICKEN DIP

1 can white meat chicken,
   drained well
1 (8 oz.) block cream cheese,
   softened

1 pkg. dried Ranch dressing
wheat crackers

Mix first 3 ingredients well. Cover and refrigerate overnight (or at least 4 hours). Serve with wheat crackers.

Jodi Sears

*C*ORN DIP

2 c. shredded Pepper Jack
   cheese
1 c. shredded Parmesan
   cheese
1 c. mayonnaise

2 cans Mexican corn,
   drained
½ jar jalapeno peppers,
   diced

Mix all ingredients and put into a dish and bake at 350° for 25 minutes. Serve hot with scoop style corn chips.

Emily Jobe

*C*ORN SALSA DIP

1 can white Shoepeg corn,
   drained well
1 can Ro-Tel tomatoes

1 (8 oz.) block cream cheese,
   softened

Mix ingredients and heat.

Gini Mizelle

CREAM CHEESE SPREAD

2 (8 oz.) cream cheese blocks,
 softened
¼ c. honey
8 oz. Cheddar cheese,
 shredded

1 (4.5 oz.) can chopped
 jalapenos, drained
10 to 12 slices bacon,
 crumbled
4 to 6 green onions, chopped

Mix all ingredients together and refrigerate for at least 1 hour.
Serve with crackers.

Amanda Locke

CRUNCHY PEANUT BUTTER-YOGURT DIP

1 (8 oz.) container honey nut
 cream cheese, softened
¾ c. creamy peanut butter
½ c. vanilla flavored yogurt
½ c. honey

1 c. granola cereal
⅛ tsp. ground nutmeg
⅛ tsp. ground cinnamon
fresh strawberries, grapes,
 sliced apples

In a medium bowl, combine cream cheese and peanut butter;
beat at medium speed with an electric mixer until creamy. Add
yogurt and honey, mixing to combine. Stir in cereal, nutmeg and cinnamon. Serve with strawberries, grapes and apples.
Note: Dip can be stored and chilled in an airtight container for
up to 5 days.

Jamie Morgan
Honorary Member

FRENCH QUARTER CHEESE SPREAD

1 (8 oz.) cream cheese,
 softened
1 Tbsp. grated onion
1 clove minced garlic
¼ c. dark brown sugar

½ stick butter
1 tsp. Worcestershire sauce
½ tsp. mustard
1 c. finely chopped pecans

Mix together the first 3 ingredients and form. Cover and chill
for at least 1 hour. Combine the next 5 ingredients in a pan and cook
over medium heat until sugar has dissolved. Pour on top of cream
cheese and cover. Refrigerate until ready to serve. Serve with
crackers.

Emily Jobe

FRUIT SALSA

strawberries, apples, kiwifruit (1 c. each), diced very small (vary amount of each by preference)	flour tortillas (large) cooking spray (butter flavored) sugar
strawberry preserves or jelly	cinnamon

Place diced fruit in a bowl. Add entire jar of strawberry preserves (size of jar is determined based on how much fruit you cut up, roughly 2 cups). Refrigerate.

Mix equal parts of cinnamon and sugar in a bowl. Set aside. Take large flour tortillas cut into triangles. Spray with butter flavored cooking spray. Sprinkle the cinnamon/sugar mixture over sprayed area. Bake at 350° until toasted.

Cheryl Young
Honorary Member

HAM ASPARAGUS ROLL UPS

1 (8 oz.) pkg. cream cheese, softened	dash of dry mustard (optional)
1 Tbsp. mayonnaise	3 (8 oz.) pkg. sliced ham
2 tsp. Worcestershire sauce	1 (15 oz.) can asparagus spears (extra long)

Cream together cream cheese, mayonnaise, Worcestershire and dry mustard. Spread 2 teaspoons of creamed mixture on dried ham slice. Roll asparagus spear in ham. Slice into desired size. Secure with toothpick.

Judy Bishop
Honorary Member

HOAGIE DIP

1 medium onion	¼ lb. deli sliced Provolone cheese
½ head iceberg lettuce	banana peppers to taste
¼ lb. deli sliced ham	1 large tomato, chopped
¼ lb. deli sliced turkey	

Dressing:

1 Tbsp. olive oil	½ c. mayo
1 ½ tsp. red pepper flakes	1 tsp. oregano

Chop veggies, meat and cheese; pour dressing over when ready to serve. Serve with thin bagels cut into quarters.

Jennifer Stanley

ℋOT PIZZA DIP

8 oz. cream cheese, softened
1 (7 oz.) jar pizza sauce
1 small onion
8 to 12 oz. shredded pizza
   cheese

3 oz. chopped pepperoni
½ lb. sausage, cooked and
   chopped
1 bag sturdy corn chips

Preheat oven to 350°. Grease the bottom of a 9-inch round pan. Brown the sausage and set aside. Spread the softened cream cheese onto the bottom of the 9-inch baking dish. Layer the other ingredients in the order listed. Bake at 350° for 20 minutes or until bubbles. Serve with sturdy chips of choice.

Julie Pennington

ℋOT SWEET ONION DIP

1 c. chopped sweet onions
1 c. light Miracle Whip

1 c. Cheddar cheese,
   shredded
pinch of kosher salt

Mix all ingredients together and bake at 350° for 20 minutes. Serve with corn chips or baked pita chips.

Millie Cline

𝒥ULIE'S SPICY CHEESE DIP

1 lb. hot sausage
1 lb. ground hamburger

1 pkg. Mexican Velveeta
1 jar medium salsa

Brown the sausage and hamburger together and drain excess grease. Cube the Velveeta and melt in the pan with the browned meat. Once fully melted, stir in the salsa. Serve with tortilla chips.
   To make an extra hot version: Use a jar of hot salsa and add 1 teaspoon crushed red pepper flakes.

Julie Pennington

𝒦IM ADAMS' EMMAUS MEATBALLS

4 Tbsp. butter or margarine
¼ c. finely chopped onions
2 c. ketchup

1 c. grape jelly
30 to 34 count frozen regular
   style meatballs

Melt butter in large skillet. Sauté onions in butter until translucent, not brown. Combine ketchup, jelly and onion in large skillet and bring to a boil. Place frozen meatballs in a crock-pot on low to medium heat. Then add the mixture that has already been brought to a boil in the crock-pot with meatballs. Simmer on low heat. Serve when ready.

Cookbook Committee

$\mathscr{M}$ABE'S CHEESE SPREAD

1 (8 oz.) cream cheese,
  softened
½ c. mayonnaise
½ c. milk

1 regular packet Hidden
  Valley dressing mix
8 oz. finely shredded sharp
  Cheddar cheese

Mix the first 4 ingredients together until creamy. Add sharp cheese to mixture. Chill in the refrigerator for at least a few hours. Serve with crackers.

Susan Ikerd

$\mathscr{M}$ARINATED CHEESE

1 (0.7 oz.) envelope Italian
  dressing mix
½ c. vegetable oil
¼ c. white vinegar
2 Tbsp. minced green onion
2 Tbsp. water
1 ½ tsp. sugar
1 (8 oz.) block Monterey Jack
  cheese, chilled

1 (8 oz.) block Cheddar
  cheese, chilled
1 (8 oz.) pkg. cream cheese,
  chilled
1 (4 oz.) jar chopped
  pimentos, drained
assorted crackers

Whisk together first 6 ingredients. Set aside. Cut Monterey Jack cheese in half lengthwise. Cut each half crosswise into ¼-inch thick slices. These will resemble a square. Repeat with Cheddar cheese and cream cheese. Arrange cheese in 4 rows in a shallow baking dish, alternating Monterey Jack cheese, Cheddar cheese and cream cheese. Pour marinade over cheese. Cover and chill at least 8 hours.

Drain marinade from cheese and arrange cheese slices on a platter in rows. Top with pimentos and serve with assorted crackers.

Emily Jobe

$\mathscr{M}$ARTHA NICHOLS' JALAPENO COCKTAIL PIE

2 or 3 jalapeno peppers,
  seeded and chopped

1 lb. sharp Cheddar cheese,
  shredded
6 eggs, beaten

Sprinkle peppers in a well-greased 9-inch square pan; cover with cheese. Pour eggs over cheese. Bake at 350° for 30 minutes or until firm. Cool and cut into 1-inch squares.

Letitia Cline
Honorary Member

ORANGE CREAMSICLE FRUIT DIP

7 oz. tub marshmallow cream
8 oz. cream cheese, softened

2 Tbsp. orange juice
concentrate

Spoon marshmallow cream into a large microwave-safe bowl. Microwave for 20 seconds so it is smooth and not so sticky. Add in the cream cheese, and then drizzle in the orange juice concentrate. Whisk until the mixture is smooth. Serve with fruit.

Laura Stanley

ORIENTAL MEATBALLS

1 ½ lb. ground beef chuck
¾ c. water chestnuts, finely
   chopped
2 Tbsp. onion, grated
¼ c. dry bread crumbs
1 egg
salt and pepper to taste

¼ c. soy sauce
½ c. pineapple juice
½ c. dry sherry
2 Tbsp. brown sugar
¼ tsp. ginger
1 Tbsp. cornstarch
½ c. chicken broth

Mix together beef, water chestnuts, onion, crumbs, egg, salt and pepper to taste. Form into balls about 1-inch in diameter. Place slightly apart on greased cookie sheet. Bake uncovered at 450° for 8 to 10 minutes or until lightly browned. (Cover and chill if made ahead.) Stir together soy sauce, pineapple juice, sherry, sugar and ginger in a wide saucepan. Add meatballs; simmer 15 minutes. Stir until slightly thickened. Keep meatballs warm in chafing dish.

Judy Bishop
Honorary Member

PIMENTO CHEESE

1 (8 oz.) block cream cheese
   (room temperature)
2 c. grated sharp Cheddar
2 c. grated Monterey Jack
1 c. Hellmann's mayonnaise
¼ tsp. salt or to taste

¼ tsp. garlic powder or to
   taste
1 tsp. grated onion
cracked black pepper
1 small container chopped
   pimentos, drained well and
   smashed

With an electric hand mixer or stand mixer, beat cream cheese until smooth and fluffy. Add everything, except pimentos, and mix until well blended and creamy. Stir in pimentos. Taste and add seasoning if needed. Place in an airtight container in the refrigerator. Use as a dip for veggies or crackers or on bread for a yummy sandwich.

Bonny Spears

*P*UFFED SAUSAGE BITES

2 cans crescent rolls	**1 lb. sausage**
2 c. shredded Cheddar cheese	**1 (8 oz.) pkg. cream cheese**

Preheat oven to 350°. Grease a 9 x 13 baking pan. Cook the sausage until no longer pink and drain grease. Add the cream cheese to the sausage mixture and heat on low until the mixture is combined.

Unroll one package of the crescent rolls and place on the bottom of the 9 x 13 pan, pressing down to cover pan. Place the sausage/cream cheese mixture over the crescent roll layer. Unroll the remaining crescent roll package and place on top of the sausage and cheese mixture. Press down slightly. Bake at 350° for 25 to 30 minutes or until lightly golden brown.

Julie Pennington

*S*AUSAGE BALLS

1 lb. hot sausage (uncooked)	**1 ¼ c. Bisquick**
8 oz. cream cheese, softened	**4 oz. Cheddar cheese**

Preheat oven to 400°. Combine all ingredients. Pinch off enough to make 1-inch balls. Bake for 10 to 12 minutes.

Laura Stanley

*S*PICY BLACK BEAN DIP

1 (15 oz.) can black beans, rinsed and drained	**1 green bell pepper, chopped to taste**
1 (15 ¼ oz.) can whole kernel corn, drained	**garlic salt to taste**
1 (10 oz.) can diced tomatoes with green chilies, drained	**1 (8 oz.) bottle Italian salad dressing**
1 small purple onion, chopped to taste	**tortilla chips**

Mix all ingredients in a bowl. Let marinate in dressing for 2 to 4 hours. Serve with chips. You may need to drain excess liquid before serving.

Beth Johnston
Honorary Member

$\mathcal{S}$PICY MARMALADE MEATBALLS

2 lb. fully cooked frozen
  meatballs
16 oz. bottle Catalina salad
  dressing

1 c. orange marmalade
3 Tbsp. Worcestershire sauce
1 tsp. red pepper flakes

Place frozen meatballs in a crock-pot. In a bowl, combine and stir remaining ingredients. Pour mixture over meatballs and stir to coat. Cook on high for 2 to 3 hours.

Melissa Auringer

$\mathcal{S}$PINACH ARTICHOKE DIP

1 (10 oz.) pkg. frozen chopped
  spinach
14 oz. can quartered
  artichoke hearts
½ c. mayonnaise
8 oz. sour cream

1 c. freshly grated Parmesan
  cheese
1 Alouette Garlic and Herb
  Spreadable Gourmet cheese
2 oz. jar pimentos
6 bacon slices, cooked and
  crumbled

Preheat oven to 400°. Defrost spinach and remove water. Stir together all ingredients, except bacon. Spoon into a lightly greased 11 x 7 baking dish. Bake at 400° for 20 minutes or until bubbly. Sprinkle with bacon. Serve with crackers or chips.

Janet Roach
Honorary Member

$\mathcal{T}$ACO DIP

8 oz. sour cream
8 oz. cream cheese
1 pkg. taco seasoning mix

4 c. grated Cheddar cheese
1 small jar salsa

Mix sour cream, cream cheese, taco mix and 2 cups of Cheddar cheese together. Place into a serving dish or mound onto a serving platter. Chill for 30 minutes. When ready to serve, top with jar of salsa and 2 more cups of Cheddar cheese. Serve with tortilla chips.

Stephanie Bagwell

$\mathcal{T}$HE BEST SALSA

1 can (28 oz.) whole tomatoes
  with juice
2 cans (10 oz.) Ro-Tel
  tomatoes with green chilies
¼ c. chopped onion
1 clove garlic, minced

2 Tbsp. jalapenos, diced
¼ tsp. sugar
¼ tsp. salt
¼ tsp. ground cumin
½ c. cilantro
½ lime, juiced

Combine all ingredients in a blender and pulse about 10 to 15 pulses and then add more cilantro and jalapenos to taste if needed. Refrigerate salsa for at least an hour. Serve with tortilla chips.

Emily Jobe

soups
Salads
& sauces

Salads

Salads can be a good source of vitamins, minerals, and fiber. Follow these suggestions when including salads as a part of your family's well-balanced diet:

- Iceberg lettuce has few nutrients. Substitute a variety of types of lettuce such as raddichio, Boston, and Romaine.
- Avocados and olives are high in fat. Use these sparingly in salads.
- Cheeses also add fat to salads.
- Season salads with herbs instead of salt.
- Use low-fat or no fat dressings; limit other dressings to 1 tablespoon.
- Substitute yogurt for sour cream in homemade dressings.
- Substitute low-fat or no fat mayonnaise when making potato salad.
- Pickles and olives are high in salt. Use sparingly.

Additions and Garnishes	Tips For Tossed Salads
Sliced Hard-Cooked Eggs - remove yolks, which are high in cholesterol	Wash greens, drain and dry well prior to storing.
Pimento	Tear greens instead of cutting to avoid bruising with a knife.
Radishes	
Green Pepper	Remove the waxy outer skin of cucumbers before slicing.
Chicken	
Carrots	Marinate tomato wedges separately in a vinaigrette; then add to salad.
Celery	
Tomatoes	
Cooked Beets	To core lettuce, smack head down hard on counter top. Then twist core out.
Cauliflower	
Broccoli	

- Remember to use low-fat or fat-free crackers as an accompaniment to salads!
- Check the labels on soups for ingredients you wish to avoid. Many commercially prepared soups are very high in salt and fat.
- When preparing homemade soups, use margarine instead of butter and herbs instead of salt.
- Many recipes call for milk as an ingredient for soups and sauces. Use skim milk or 1% if possible.
- When preparing dressings, use vegetable oils such as olive, sunflower or canola. These contain less fat and as with all vegetable oils … they contain no cholesterol!

SOUPS, SALADS & SAUCES

BEEF STEW

(Low-Fat)

½ lb. boneless beef sirloin
  steak (½-inch thick), fat
  trimmed
2 small red potatoes, cubed
½ pkg. (from 16 oz. pkg.)
  peeled baby carrots

½ jar (from 12 oz. jar) beef
  gravy
½ tsp. onion salt
¼ tsp. black pepper

You will need 2 sheets (12 x 18-inches each) heavy-duty aluminum foil.

Preheat oven to 450° or grill to medium-high. Spray foil with nonstick spray. Cut steak in ½-inch cubes. Center half of beef, potatoes and carrots in an even layer on each sheet of aluminum foil. Spoon gravy over beef mixture; sprinkle with onion salt and pepper. Bring up foil sides. Double fold top and ends to seal packet, leaving room for heat circulation inside. Repeat to make two packets. Bake 30 to 35 minutes on a cookie sheet in oven or grill 14 to 16 minutes in covered grill. Stir before serving.

Delane Stevens

BROCCOLI CHOWDER

2 lb. fresh broccoli
2 (13 ¾ oz.) cans chicken
  broth, divided
3 c. milk
1 c. cooked ham, chopped
2 tsp. salt

¼ tsp. pepper
1 c. half and half
2 c. (½ lb.) Swiss cheese,
  shredded
¼ c. margarine

Combine broccoli and 1 can chicken broth in a Dutch oven; cover and cook 7 minutes or until broccoli is crisp-tender. Remove broccoli from broth; cool and chop coarsely. Add remaining can of chicken broth, milk, ham, salt and pepper to Dutch oven; bring to boil over medium heat, stirring occasionally. Stir in broccoli and remaining ingredients. Cook over low heat until thoroughly heated but do not boil.

Ann Fincher
Honorary Member

$\mathcal{B}$ROCCOLI WILD RICE SOUP

1 (6 oz.) pkg. chicken and
   wild rice mix
5 c. water
1 (10 oz.) pkg. frozen chopped
   broccoli, thawed
1 medium carrot, shredded

2 tsp. dried minced onion
1 can (10 ¾ oz.) condensed
   cream of chicken soup
   (undiluted)
1 (8 oz.) pkg. cream cheese,
   cubed

In a large saucepan combine rice, contents of seasoning package and water; bring to a boil. Reduce heat; cover and simmer for 10 minutes, stirring once. Stir in the broccoli, carrot and onion. Cover and simmer for 5 to 10 minutes (whenever carrots become tender). Stir in soup and cream cheese. Cook and stir until cheese is melted. Makes 12 servings (3 quarts).

If reheated at a later time, you may want to add some chicken broth, as it will become thicker.

Jamie Morgan
Honorary Member

$\mathcal{B}$RUNSWICK STEW

1 medium onion
2 (28 oz.) cans diced
   tomatoes
2 (10 oz.) cans chicken (white
   meat)
2 (10 oz.) cans barbecued
   pork
2 (10 oz.) cans barbecued
   beef

1 tsp. sugar
1 (14 ¾ oz.) can cream style
   sweet yellow corn
1 (15 oz.) can Shoe Peg white
   corn
½ c. barbecue sauce
1 heaping tsp. black pepper
1 tsp. salt
2 Tbsp. white vinegar

Process onion, tomatoes and chicken in food processor until nearly smooth (not pureed). Mix all ingredients in slow cooker or on stove top on low/simmer for 6 to 8 hours, stirring occasionally.

Stephanie Bagwell

$\mathcal{C}$HEESE SOUP

2 to 3 cans chicken broth
   (depending on how thick
   you like your soup)
2 cans Ro-Tel (1 can ½
   drained)
1 large block Velveeta, cubed

1 ½ to 2 lb. meat (can be
   ground meat, turkey,
   chicken, sausage, etc.)
1 bag frozen vegetables
   (broccoli and cauliflower
   are good)
1 can black beans, rinsed
   and drained

Brown meat and drain. Combine remaining ingredients. Heat through, stirring occasionally.

Jory Cannon
Honorary Member

*C*HEF MICHAEL'S ROASTED BUTTERNUT SQUASH SOUP

1 large butternut squash (around 4 lb.)	2 bay leaves
2 medium onions	2 c. half and half
4 Tbsp. olive oil	½ tsp. garlic powder
4 c. vegetable stock	2 tsp. salt
¾ tsp. cinnamon	¼ tsp. freshly ground nutmeg
½ tsp. light chili powder	(½ tsp. if preground)
1 ½ tsp. thyme	white pepper to taste

Roast onions and squash after tossing with olive oil for 45 minutes. Place onions and squash into a large soup pot with vegetable stock, cinnamon, bay leaves, chili powder and thyme. Simmer 45 minutes. Remove from heat.

Using an immersion (stick) blender, puree all ingredients until smooth. If you don't have an immersion blender, puree ingredients in small batches using a regular blender or food processor. Add half and half and continue to puree until creamy. Add garlic, salt, nutmeg and pepper and return to a simmer for 5 minutes. Adjust seasonings to taste and remove to cool.

Lisa Woodruff

*C*HICKEN TORTILLA SOUP

6 Tbsp. olive oil	6 c. chicken broth
6 cloves garlic, minced	1 tsp. salt
½ c. chopped fresh cilantro	½ tsp. cayenne pepper
1 medium onion, chopped	1 zucchini or yellow squash,
1 can (28 oz.) diced tomatoes	chunked
1 Tbsp. chili powder	4 to 6 cooked chicken
1 Tbsp. ground cumin	breasts, shredded or cubed
3 bay leaves	

Garnish:

Monterey Jack cheese	2 corn tortillas, sliced and
avocado, cubed	fried crisp
sour cream	

Heat oil in a large saucepan over medium heat. Add garlic, cilantro and onion and sauté 2 to 3 minutes. Stir in tomatoes. Bring to a boil and add cumin, chili powder, bay leaves and chicken stock. Return to a boil. Reduce heat and add salt and cayenne. Simmer 30 minutes. Remove bay leaves and stir in the chicken and the squash. Simmer 10 minutes. Garnish with Monterey Jack, avocado, sour cream and toasted tortilla strips.

Ann Fincher
Honorary Member

ROBYN'S CHICKEN TORTILLA SOUP

½ c. chopped onion
½ c. chopped green bell
  pepper
1 Tbsp. olive oil
3 to 4 boneless chicken
  breasts, cooked, drained
  and chopped
1 (15 oz.) can whole kernel
  corn, drained
1 (15 oz.) can black beans,
  drained and rinsed
1 (15 oz.) can kidney beans,
  drained and rinsed
1 (10 oz.) Ro-Tel tomatoes
  (mild or original)
2 or 3 (14 oz.) cans chicken
  broth, divided
1 (1 oz.) pkg. taco seasoning
1 (1 oz.) pkg. Ranch dressing
  mix
salt and pepper to taste

Sauté the first 3 ingredients until tender. Melt 1 (10 ounce) block of Velveeta and ½ cup chicken broth in microwave, stirring occasionally to prevent burning. Pour into crock-pot along with all the other ingredients. Simmer for 2 hours. Change the consistency of the soup by adding more of the third can of broth if desired. Serve hot with corn chips.

Robyn McEntyre

SPICY ROTISSERIE CHICKEN SOUP

1 small yellow onion, diced
1 small can mushrooms
olive oil to taste
1 small can Niblets corn
1 Tbsp. butter
1 Tbsp. garlic, minced
2 Tbsp. Zesty Italian
  dressing
dash of lemon juice
½ tsp. Caribbean Jerk
  seasoning
dash of red pepper flakes
¼ tsp. garlic salt
¼ tsp. parsley flakes
¼ tsp. black pepper
1 can Ro-Tel tomatoes
32 oz. low sodium chicken
  broth
½ rotisserie chicken,
  shredded (Mojo flavored if
  available)

Microwave the onions in 1 cup of water for 2 minutes; then drain. Sauté onions and mushrooms with olive oil for 5 minutes. Add corn, butter, garlic, Italian dressing, lemon juice and all seasonings. Add chicken. Sauté for 10 minutes in skillet on low heat. Puree Ro-Tel tomatoes. Add tomato mixture and chicken broth to a medium sized stockpot. Bring to a boil. Add all ingredients from skillet to stockpot. Cook uncovered on low heat for 15 minutes.

Angela Wilson

$\mathcal{S}$LOW COOKER CHICKEN, TURKEY AND WHITE BEAN CHILI

1 lb. chicken sausage
1 lb. ground turkey breast
2 onions, chopped
4 cloves garlic, minced
2 (15 oz. each) cans cannellini beans, drained
1 (29 oz.) can hominy, drained
3 (14 oz.) cans low sodium chicken broth
¼ c. fresh cilantro
1 ½ tsp. ground cumin
1 tsp. Cajun seasoning
1 tsp. jerk seasoning

Remove casing of sausage and brown chicken and turkey in skillet. Drain and put meat into a bowl; set aside. In same skillet, cook the onion and garlic over medium heat until the onion is translucent, about 5 minutes. Scrape onions and garlic and any remaining drippings into the bowl with the meat.

Place 2 cans of cannellini beans, hominy and the chicken broth into a slow cooker. Transfer the browned meat mixture and remaining seasonings into the slow cooker and stir to combine. Cover and cook on low for 4 to 6 hours or high for 2 to 3 hours.

Garnish as desired using: yogurt, sour cream, peach or mango salsa, avocado, lime juice, cheese or fresh cilantro. If you want thicker chili, puree up to 3 cans of beans until smooth and add to the crock-pot with the chicken broth.

Deanna Adkins

$\mathcal{C}$ORN CHOWDER

2 (16 oz.) cans whole kernel corn, drained
2 to 3 medium baking potatoes, chopped
2 c. chicken broth
2 c. whole milk or half and half
¼ c. butter, softened
½ tsp. salt
pepper to taste

Place drained corn, chicken broth, salt and pepper in a blender and puree. Add butter and milk. Put the mixture in a crock-pot. Cook for 4 hours on low.

Add chopped potatoes to a saucepan with water and bring to a boil. Once the potatoes are tender (approximately 20 minutes), mash them up and add to the corn chowder in hot crock-pot. Cook for an additional hour.

Laura Stanley

MARYLAND CRAB-SWEET CORN CHOWDER

1 ½ c. frozen whole kernel
   corn
1 medium finely chopped
   onion
2 cloves minced garlic
1 tsp. cooking oil
14 ½ oz. can chicken broth
1 c. whipping cream
⅛ tsp. salt

⅛ tsp. white pepper
1 medium chopped potato
¼ c. finely chopped red,
   yellow or green sweet
   pepper
6 oz. fresh or frozen cooked
   crabmeat
fresh parsley

In a 2-quart saucepan cook half of the whole kernel corn, the onion and garlic in hot cooking oil until onion is tender but not brown. Carefully add chicken broth. Bring to boiling; reduce heat. Simmer, uncovered, for 10 minutes. Stir in whipping cream, salt and white pepper. Simmer, uncovered, for 10 minutes or until slightly thickened. (Watch carefully because it may foam and rise in the pan.) Remove from heat; cool slightly. Pour the cooled mixture into a blender. Cover and blend until smooth. Return to the same saucepan; keep warm.

Meanwhile, in a small covered saucepan cook remaining corn and potato in boiling salted water for 2 minutes. Add chopped sweet pepper. Cover and cook about 1 minute more or until tender. Drain. Stir the drained vegetables into the soup. Add the fresh or frozen crabmeat; heat through. If desired, garnish each serving with parsley and red pepper strips.

JoAnne Knieriem

BAKED POTATO SOUP

¼ c. butter or margarine
¼ c. onion, chopped
¼ c. all-purpose flour
14.5 oz. can chicken broth
12 oz. can evaporated milk

2 to 3 large baking potatoes,
   baked
cooked and crumbled bacon
   (optional)
shredded Cheddar cheese
   (optional)

Melt butter in a large saucepan over medium heat. Add onion; cook, stirring occasionally, for 1 to 2 minutes or until tender. Stir in flour. Gradually stir in broth and evaporated milk. Scoop potato pulp from 1 potato (reserve potato skin), until mixture comes just to a boil. Dice remaining potato skin and potato(es); add to soup. Season with salt and ground black pepper. Top each serving with bacon and cheese if desired.

Laura Stanley

CROCK-POT POTATO SOUP

1 (30 oz.) bag frozen
   shredded or cubed hash
   browns
3 (14 oz.) cans chicken broth
1 (10.75 oz.) can cream of
   chicken soup
½ chopped onion
¼ tsp. ground black pepper
1 (8 oz.) pkg. cream cheese,
   softened

In a 6-quart crock-pot, combine potatoes, broth, soup, onion and pepper. Cover and cook on low for 5 hours. Stir in cream cheese and cook for an additional 30 minutes, until combined.

Emily Jobe

SPECIAL POTATO SOUP

1 medium onion, chopped
2 celery stalks, chopped
2 tsp. butter
6 medium to large white
   potatoes, cubed
2 carrots, sliced thin
1 tsp. garlic
3 c. water
¾ tsp. Lawry's seasoned salt
½ tsp. dry thyme
a dash of pepper
5 chicken bouillon cubes
2 c. milk
1 c. shredded Cheddar cheese

Sauté the onion and celery in butter until tender. Add the remaining ingredients, except milk and cheese. Cook for approximately 1 hour over medium heat until potatoes and carrots are tender. Remove soup mixture from heat. Use a vegetable masher to mash up part of the soup if desired. Add milk to soup. Gradually stir in cheese until well blended and cheese is melted.

Wendy Landry

CHUCK'S VEGETABLE SOUP

1 lb. lean ground beef, browned
1 can Ro-Tel tomatoes, pureed
42 oz. can tomato juice
16 oz. can pureed tomatoes
½ head cabbage, chopped
2 baking potatoes, cubed
1 medium onion (white or yellow), diced
½ stick butter
1 tsp. garlic paste
1 bouillon cube (chicken or beef)
32 oz. low sodium chicken broth
1 c. frozen butter beans
1 Tbsp. sugar
½ Tbsp. pepper
1 can black-eyed peas, drained and rinsed
½ c. frozen green peas

In a large stockpot, combine chicken broth, tomato juice, cabbage and potatoes. Cook for 25 minutes on medium heat. While mixture is cooking, place onions in a microwave-safe container. Cover with water and cook in the microwave for 2 minutes; drain. Add with remaining ingredients to the stockpot. Cook for another 30 minutes on medium heat, stirring frequently.

Angela Wilson

GOOP SOUP

2 lb. ground beef
1 small sweet onion, diced
1 Tbsp. olive oil
1 can Ro-Tel (flavor to taste)
2 cans Ranch Style beans
1 can Niblets corn, drained
1 can dark kidney beans, drained
½ small packet Ranch dry dressing mix
1 ½ packets chili seasoning
1 lb. Velveeta, cut into chunks
1 pt. half and half
Goop to taste

Put olive oil in large pot. Add onions and cook until begin to soften. Add ground beef and cook until browned. Drain off fat. Add Ro-Tel, Ranch Style beans, kidney beans, corn, Ranch dressing mix and chili seasoning. Mix well; then allow to simmer on low, stirring occasionally. Simmer could last 30 minutes to 2 hours. Add Velveeta and stir to make sure cheese is fully melted and integrated. Turn heat to low. Approximately 30 minutes before serving, add the half and half and stir frequently. Turn heat up a "tad" just to get steaming again.

Serve with "Goop" of your choice: jalapenos, avocado slices, shredded lettuce, sour cream, shredded cheese, corn chips, etc. This recipe is also great with corn bread or over baked potatoes.

Molly Mercer

$\mathcal{P}$ASTA FAGIOLI SOUP

1 ½ to 2 tsp. olive oil
1 ½ lb. lean ground beef
1 to 2 onions, chopped to
  your liking
1 pkg. shredded carrots or
  julienned
7 oz. celery, sliced thin
24 oz. canned diced tomatoes
1 can red kidney beans,
  drained and rinsed
1 can white kidney beans,
  drained and rinsed

44 oz. beef stock (plus or
  minus)
1 ½ tsp. oregano
1 ¼ tsp. pepper
2 ½ tsp. parsley (fresh or
  dried)
¾ tsp. Tabasco sauce
24 oz. spaghetti sauce
  (Hunt's canned four cheese
  flavor)
8 oz. ditalini pasta
Parmesan cheese

Sauté beef in olive oil in a large soup pot until meat starts to brown. Add onions, carrots, celery and tomatoes and simmer for about 10 minutes. Add rinsed beans, beef stock, oregano, pepper, parsley, Tabasco and spaghetti sauce. Simmer until vegetables are tender, at least 45 minutes. Add ditalini pasta and cook until pasta is tender. Serve with freshly grated Parmesan cheese on top and crusty bread.

Bonny Spears

$\mathcal{T}$ACO SOUP

1 lb. ground beef
1 large onion, diced
3 (16 oz.) chili beans
  (undrained)
2 (16 oz.) diced tomatoes
  (undrained)

1 (16 oz.) tomato sauce
1 (4.5 oz.) green chilies,
  chopped
1 pkg. taco seasoning
1 pkg. Ranch dressing mix
1 ½ c. water

Brown ground beef until fully cooked. Combine all of the ingredients into crock-pot and cook on low for 4 to 6 hours. Serve with shredded cheese, sour cream, tortilla chips and jalapenos if desired.

Emily Jobe

TURKEY CHILI

1 sweet onion, chopped
2 to 3 stalks celery, sliced
　　thin
2 cloves garlic
1 lb. ground turkey
1 carton turkey or chicken
　　stock
1 can fire roasted green
　　chilies

1 jar salsa verde
1 tsp. dried oregano
½ tsp. fresh ground pepper
½ tsp. dried cilantro
pinch of red pepper flakes
1 bag of dry white
　　kidney/cannellini beans

Sauté chopped onion and celery until translucent in olive oil. When this is almost done, press 2 medium cloves of garlic into mixture. Cook for a couple minutes until garlic is done. Remove from pan. In same pan, sauté ground turkey until no longer pink. Add the celery, onion and garlic mixture back into pan. Stir together until heated through.

Transfer mixture to a stockpot. Add carton of stock, fire roasted green chilies, salsa verde and spices. Bring mixture to a boil; then immediately reduce to low and cook for about 20 minutes. Pour into crock-pot crock and add 1 bag of rinsed dry white kidney/cannellini beans and place the whole crock into fridge overnight. The next morning add about 10 ice cubes and turn crock-pot on low. Eight to ten hours later...Yum!

Serve with sour cream, fresh cilantro, Monterey Jack cheese and tortilla chips!

Note: If you desire to eat this immediately, you can add 2 cans of cannellini beans to the stockpot and omit the crock-pot stage.

Bonny Spears

TUSCAN SOUP

3 cloves garlic, smashed
1 small onion, chopped
1 carrot, chopped
1 celery stalk, chopped
4 oz. pancetta or ham
2 Tbsp. olive oil
15 oz. can whole tomatoes

3 (15 oz.) cans cannellini or
　　navy beans, rinsed and
　　drained
2 c. chicken broth
1 sprig fresh rosemary
1 bunch fresh kale, chopped
½ c. toasted bread crumbs
Garnish: grated Parmesan
　　cheese

Heat the first 5 ingredients in 2 tablespoons olive oil for about 5 minutes. Add tomatoes, beans, broth and rosemary and simmer 1 hour. Add kale and cook 5 to 7 minutes. Stir in the bread crumbs. Garnish each bowl with Parmesan. Serves 6.

Ann Fincher
Honorary Member

APPLE SALAD

1 medium Golden Delicious apple, chopped	2 celery ribs, thinly sliced
1 medium red apple, chopped	½ c. golden raisins
	¼ c. honey

In a bowl, combine the apples, celery and raisins. Add the honey and mix well. Serve immediately.

Michelle Bowden

NANNY'S APPLE SALAD

½ c. sugar	¾ c. dry roasted peanuts, coarsely ground in food processor
1 Tbsp. flour	
1 (8 oz.) can crushed pineapple (undrained)	1 large tub Cool Whip
2 tsp. apple cider vinegar	4 c. Granny Smith apples, peeled, cored and cut up

Mix first 4 ingredients and cook over medium-high heat about 20 minutes. Pour into an airtight container and refrigerate overnight.

The next day, peel, core and cut Granny Smith apples to make 4 cups. Mix with refrigerated mixture, peanuts and Cool Whip. Refrigerate until ready to serve.

Gina Mickler

PENNINGTON'S APPLE SNICKER SALAD

1 bag fun sized Snickers, chopped	12 oz. (1 ½ bars) cream cheese, softened
4 Granny Smith apples, chopped	1 small jar Marshmallow Creme
	1 tub Cool Whip, thawed

Combine the cream cheese, Cool Whip and Marshmallow Creme by hand. Add the chopped Snickers and chopped apple. Stir to combine and refrigerate until ready to serve. Stir well before serving.

Julie Pennington

BLUEBERRY SALAD

2 (3 oz.) lemon jello	8 oz. cream cheese
2 c. boiling water	½ pt. sour cream
1 (20 oz.) can crushed	½ c. sugar
pineapple	1 tsp. vanilla
1 can blueberry pie filling	½ c. nuts

Mix jello, water, pineapple and blueberry pie filling and allow to congeal. Mix together cream cheese, sour cream, sugar and vanilla; add nuts and spread over congealed mixture. Refrigerate until ready to serve.

Kim Fowler

FROZEN FRUIT SALAD

3 Tbsp. chopped maraschino	⅓ c. chopped walnuts
cherries	9 oz. can crushed pineapple,
2 c. sour cream	drained
¾ c. granulated sugar	1 medium banana, diced
2 Tbsp. lemon juice	

Line muffin pan with paper cups. Drain cherries on paper towels. Mix sour cream, sugar and lemon juice. Blend in walnuts and fruits (pineapple, cherries and banana). Spoon into baking cups and freeze. Before serving, remove paper cups and allow to stand at room temperature for a few minutes before serving.

Laura Stanley

AUNT GLADYS' FROZEN FRUIT SALAD

2 small pkg. (3 oz. each)	½ c. diced pineapple,
cream cheese	drained
1 c. mayonnaise	1 can fruit cocktail (16 or 20
1 c. heavy cream, whipped	oz. size), drained
½ c. maraschino red	2 ½ c. marshmallows, diced
cherries, quartered	(about 24 marshmallows)

Beat together the cream cheese and mayonnaise. Fold in the whipped cream, cherries, drained fruit cocktail, pineapple and marshmallows. Pour into a 1-quart freezer container. Garnish with additional maraschino cherries. Also can be frozen in lined muffin tins for individual servings. Freeze fruit salad until firm.

Jory Cannon
Honorary Member

FRUITY PASTA SALAD

1 lb. pkg. bow tie pasta
8 oz. fresh sugar snap or
   snow pea pods, trimmed
   (2 ½ c.)
2 c. cubed honeydew melon
1 c. plus creamy poppy seed
   dressing

1 ½ tsp. finely shredded
   orange peel
2 c. strawberries, hulled and
   quartered lengthwise
1 ½ c. honey roasted cashews

In a large pot, cook pasta in salted water according to the package directions, adding the pea pods to the pasta the last 1 minute of cooking. Drain pasta and pea pods. Rinse with cold water and drain again. Transfer to a very large mixing bowl. Add melon and toss to combine. In a small bowl stir together the dressing and orange peel. Add to pasta mixture and toss to coat. Cover and chill up to 24 hours.

Just before serving, gently stir in the strawberries and nuts. If necessary, stir in up to ½ cup additional poppy seed dressing to moisten. Transfer to a serving bowl.

Bonny Spears

ORANGE DELIGHT

1 large pkg. orange jello
2 c. boiling water
2 c. orange sherbet

1 small cans mandarin
   oranges, drained

Dissolve the jello in boiling water. Add the sherbet, mixing well until melted. Stir in the oranges. Pour into a 9 x 13 dish and refrigerate until set, approximately 6 to 8 hours.

Julie Pennington

GRANNY'S ORANGE DELIGHT

1 (4 ½ c. servings) pkg.
   orange jello
1 (8 oz.) container Cool Whip

1 (14.5 oz.) can pear halves
1 (8 oz.) pkg. cream cheese

Allow cream cheese to soften at room temperature. Drain pears and heat juice until boiling. Dissolve jello in the boiling pear juice. Cut cream cheese into chunks and stir into jello and pear juice over medium-high heat until smooth and creamy (no lumps). Allow this mixture to partly cool.

While it cools, finely mash pears (or use a food processor). Stir mashed pears into partly cooled cream cheese/jello mixture. Fold in Cool Whip and stir until smooth. Pour into an 8 x 8 pan and refrigerate overnight until firm.

Optional: To serve, cut into even sized squares and garnish with a dollop of Cool Whip and a mint leaf.

Millie Cline and Nellie Johnson

ORANGE FLUFF FRUIT SALAD

12 oz. light Cool Whip
2 (0.3 oz.) boxes sugar-free
  orange jello
12 oz. Light 'n Lively cottage
  cheese

20 oz. can crushed pineapple,
  drained
2 (11 oz.) cans mandarin
  oranges, drained

Combine Cool Whip and cottage cheese in large mixing bowl; sprinkle jello on top; stir until jello dissolves. Fold in well drained pineapple and oranges. Refrigerate up to 4 hours or overnight and then serve. Will keep well for several days in refrigerator.

Kim Fowler

ORANGE SHERBET SALAD

3 oz. each pkg. orange jello
1 c. boiling water
1 qt. orange sherbet
2 c. marshmallows
1 can mandarin oranges,
  drained

1 (8 oz.) can crushed
  pineapple
½ pt. whipping cream,
  lightly whipped

Blend jello and water. Add orange sherbet and marshmallows while hot. Then add other ingredients. Pour into a 13 x 9 glass dish and chill until firm. Cut into squares and serve.

Lynn Struck

AUNT DOLLY'S FIVE P SALAD

1 pkg. jello (lemon or other)
1 c. boiling water
1 small can English peas
½ c. pimento
½ c. pecans

2 spoons sweet pickles
1 small can crushed
  pineapple
celery if desired

Dissolve jello into boiling water. Mix remaining ingredients and pour into bowl to congeal.

Mary Johnston
Honorary Member

$\mathscr{M}$OM'S GREEN CONGEALED SALAD

2 cans large size pears,
  drained (reserve liquid)
  and mashed
1 large box lime jello
2 (8 oz.) pkg. softened cream
  cheese

1 (8 oz.) container thawed
  Cool Whip topping
1 c. chopped pecans
1 c. miniature marshmallows

Remove pears from cans and mash with a fork, reserving liquid. Heat 1 cup of the reserved pear juice in medium saucepan until boiling. Pour powdered lime jello in 13 x 9-inch pan. Pour boiling pear juice over powdered jello. Stir until jello is completely dissolved. Combine the packages of softened cream cheese with the jello mixture. Carefully add the pears that have been mashed well with a fork, the Cool Whip, marshmallows and pecans. Cover and chill overnight. Slice and serve.

Jodi Sears

$\mathscr{S}$TRAWBERRY PRETZEL SALAD

2 c. crushed pretzels
1 c. sugar
¾ c. melted butter
1 (8 oz.) pkg. cream cheese,
  softened

1 (16 oz.) carton Cool Whip
1 (6 oz.) pkg. strawberry
  gelatin
1 c. frozen strawberries,
  thawed

Mix the pretzel crumbs, ¼ cup sugar and butter in bowl. Press into a 9 x 13-inch pan. Bake at 400° for 10 minutes. Blend cream cheese and ¾ cup sugar. Add the whipped topping. Spread over the baked layer and place the pan in the refrigerator.

Bring 1 ½ cups of water to boil and dissolve the strawberry gelatin. Stir in the thawed strawberries and let set for 5 minutes. Remove pan from the refrigerator and spread strawberry gelatin over the cream cheese mixture. Return to refrigerator and allow to congeal for 3 to 4 hours.

Julie Pennington

KAREN'S STRAWBERRY PRETZEL SALAD

2 c. finely crushed pretzels
½ c. sugar, divided
⅔ c. butter or margarine, melted
1 ½ pkg. (8 oz. each) cream cheese, softened
2 Tbsp. milk
1 c. thawed Cool Whip
2 c. boiling water
2 (3 oz.) strawberry gelatin
1 ½ c. cold water
1 qt. (4 c.) fresh strawberries, sliced

Heat oven to 350°. Mix pretzel crumbs, ¼ cup sugar and butter; press into bottom of 13 x 9 pan. Bake 10 minutes. Cool. Beat cream cheese, remaining sugar and milk until blended. Stir in Cool Whip. Spread over crust. Refrigerate.

Add boiling water to gelatin mix in large bowl. Stir 2 minutes until completely dissolved. Stir in cold water and let sit for 5 minutes. Stir in strawberries. Refrigerate 1 ½ hours or until thickened; spoon over cream cheese layer. Refrigerate 3 hours or until firm.

Bonny Spears

ANTIPASTO SALAD

2 (6.5 oz.) jars marinated artichokes (undrained)
3 Tbsp. olive oil
2 Tbsp. white wine vinegar
1 clove garlic, minced
6 c. romaine lettuce, chopped
4 medium tomatoes, cut into wedges
1 (3.5 oz.) pkg. sliced pepperoni
8 oz. Mozzarella cheese, sliced into strips
1 small purple onion, sliced and separated
½ c. whole pitted ripe black olives
4 slices bacon, cooked and crumbled

Drain artichokes and reserve marinade. Set aside artichokes. Combine marinade, oil, vinegar and garlic in jar. Cover tightly and shake. Set aside. In a large bowl, layer lettuce, tomatoes, artichokes, pepperoni, cheese, onion and olives. Drizzle with dressing and sprinkle with bacon crumbles. Cover and chill at least 3 hours. Toss gently before serving.

Jodi Sears

*A*UTUMN CHOPPED SALAD

6 to 8 c. chopped romaine lettuce	8 slices bacon, cooked and crumbled
2 medium pears, chopped	6 oz. Feta cheese, crumbled
1 c. dried cranberries	poppy seed dressing
1 c. chopped pecans	balsamic vinaigrette

On a large platter combine the lettuce, pears, cranberries, pecans, bacon and Feta cheese. Combine the two salad dressings (approximately 1 cup of dressing: 70 percent poppy seed dressing and 30 percent balsamic vinaigrette). Drizzle over the entire salad and lightly toss.

Emily Jobe

*C*OLLEEN'S SALAD

6 to 8 c. chopped romaine lettuce	4 to 6 oz. goat cheese, crumbled
1 c. dried cranberries	½ c. poppy seed salad dressing
1 c. chopped pecans	
8 slices thick cut bacon, crisp-cooked and crumbled	½ c. balsamic vinaigrette red onion (optional)

On a large platter or in a large bowl, combine the lettuce, cranberries, pecans, bacon and goat cheese. Whisk the two dressings together and then drizzle the dressing over the salad. Toss well.
Optional: Add a small amount of red onion.

Millie Cline

*C*RANBERRY SPINACH SALAD

1 Tbsp. butter	½ c. white wine
¾ c. slivered almonds	2 tsp. minced onions
1 lb. spinach	¼ tsp. paprika
1 c. dried cranberries	¼ c. white wine vinegar
2 Tbsp. toasted sesame seed	¼ c. cider vinegar
1 Tbsp. poppy seeds	½ c. vegetable oil

In a medium saucepan melt butter over medium heat. Cook and stir almonds in butter until lightly toasted. Remove from heat and let cool. In a large bowl, combine the spinach with the toasted almonds and cranberries. In a medium bowl whisk together the sesame seed, poppy seeds, onion, paprika, both vinegars and vegetable oil. Toss with spinach just before serving.

Paula Evans

FRESH PEAR SALAD WITH ASIAN DRESSING

2 c. red cabbage, shredded
2 c. romaine lettuce, torn
   into bite size pieces
½ c. chopped carrots

3 red Bartlett pears, sliced
1 green onion, chopped
sesame seeds, toasted

Combine all salad ingredients in a large bowl or platter.

½ c. vegetable oil
4 Tbsp. white wine vinegar
2 Tbsp. soy sauce

4 tsp. sugar
½ tsp. sesame oil
½ tsp. crushed red pepper

Combine all dressing ingredients. Whisk together. Pour over salad and serve immediately.

Beth Major

GRANDMA JO'S SPINACH SALAD

1 bag baby spinach
1 small can bean sprouts,
   drained
1 small can water chestnuts,
   drained and thinly sliced
2 hard-boiled eggs, cut into
   slices

8 slices bacon, fried crisp
   and crumbled
1 small red onion, sliced
   thinly and separated into
   rings

Toss ingredients in a large bowl.

Dressing:
1 c. salad oil (vegetable or
   canola)
½ c. red wine vinegar

½ c. sugar
⅓ c. ketchup
1 dash of salt

Blend well and chill. Pour over blended greens and toss just before serving.

Bonny Spears

$\mathcal{K}$IM ADAMS' KENTUCKY SALAD WITH BACON AND DIJON DRESSING

1 head romaine lettuce
1 bag baby spinach
1 c. roasted red peppers

½ c. chilled whole corn
¼ c. green onions
¼ c. bacon bits

Combine all ingredients together in a large salad bowl.

Dijon Dressing:

2 Tbsp. sour cream
4 tsp. olive oil

2 tsp. Dijon mustard
2 Tbsp. apple cider vinegar

Mix all ingredients together and pour over salad just before serving. Toss thoroughly.

Cookbook Committee

$\mathcal{L}$ILLIAN THOMASON'S KOREAN SALAD

1 lb. fresh spinach
1 (8 oz.) can water chestnuts, drained and sliced

1 (16 oz.) can bean sprouts, drained
6 slices bacon, cooked and crumbled

Dressing:

½ c. sugar
½ c. ketchup
⅓ c. vinegar
1 c. salad oil

5 Tbsp. Worcestershire sauce
1 small onion, quartered and sliced thin

Combine spinach, water chestnuts and bean sprouts. Sprinkle with bacon. Combine remaining (dressing) ingredients in container; blend well. Pour over salad and toss lightly.

Beth Allison
Honorary Member

$\mathcal{M}$ARY LYNN'S BROCCOLI SALAD

2 bunches broccoli, cut into small pieces
1 lb. bacon, cooked and crumbled
1 c. raisins (golden are best)

1 c. green onions, chopped
2 c. mayonnaise
½ c. sugar
4 Tbsp. apple cider vinegar

Combine broccoli and bacon. Mix remaining ingredients. Chill well. Dressing may be made the day before. Add it to the broccoli and bacon before serving.

Lisa Woodruff

SWEET AND CRUNCHY BROCCOLI SALAD

1 lb. bacon	1 c. raisins
1 large head broccoli	½ c. sunflower seeds
½ head cauliflower	1 c. mayonnaise
1 medium red onion, chopped	½ c. sugar
fine	2 Tbsp. vinegar

Cook 1 pound of bacon until crisp. Drain on paper towel until cool and crumble into small pieces. Chop flowerets of broccoli and cauliflower into ½-inch chunks; discard stems. Slice onion thinly and chop up fine; add to vegetables. Mix in the raisins and sunflower seeds.

In a separate bowl, combine mayonnaise, sugar and vinegar. Add to vegetable mixture. Toss to coat. Chill and serve.

Flavors are best when they have time to marry. This is a great salad to make the night before a gathering.

Bonny Spears

CALICO SALAD

1 can white whole kernel	1 jar pimento
corn	1 sliced bell pepper
1 can English peas	1 c. diced celery
1 can French-style green	1 c. diced onion
beans	

Drain these vegetables; place in bowl.

1 tsp. salt	1 Tbsp. water
½ tsp. pepper	½ c. oil
1 c. sugar	¾ c. vinegar

Mix ingredients and heat. Pour over vegetables at least 4 hours before serving.

Kim Fowler

COLD PEA SALAD

1 head lettuce
2 pkg. (10 oz. each) frozen
   peas, barely cooked and
   drained
1 small red onion, very finely
   sliced
½ c. chopped celery
5 carrots, grated

4 Tbsp. chopped fresh parsley
½ tsp. salt
½ tsp. pepper
2 c. sour cream
2 c. Hellmann's mayonnaise
½ lb. bacon, cooked and set
   aside

Wash lettuce thoroughly. Remove stem and tear into bite size pieces. Dry thoroughly with a lettuce spinner or roll in a clean kitchen towel and squeeze out excess water. Set in refrigerator for an hour.

In a large clear glass bowl, layer washed and thoroughly dried lettuce, peas and onions. Combine parsley and celery on top of onion layer. Mix salt, pepper, sour cream and mayonnaise. Spread over salad, sealing to the edges of your bowl. Cover with plastic wrap and chill overnight. Place crumbled bacon on top just before serving.

Bonny Spears

CHICKEN SALAD

2 ½ c. chicken, cooked and
   diced
1 c. celery, chopped
1 Tbsp. lemon juice
½ tsp. salt and pepper

½ c. mayonnaise
1 small onion, chopped
1 tsp. Worcestershire sauce
1 c. seedless grapes, halved

Mix all ingredients together. Chill 2 hours or longer.

Robyn McEntyre

KIM ADAMS' CHICKEN ARTICHOKE SALAD

1 ½ c. cooked and chopped
   chicken
1 c. shredded Parmesan
   cheese
1 c. quartered red grapes
½ c. finely chopped pecans
½ Tbsp. lemon juice

½ tsp. pepper
8 oz. pkg. cream cheese,
   softened
7 oz. jar artichoke hearts,
   drained and chopped
2 green onions, chopped
¼ tsp. salt

Mix all ingredients together. Serve as cracker spread or as sandwiches.

Cookbook Committee

COLESLAW

1 pkg. shredded cabbage
½ green pepper, chopped
½ red pepper, chopped
1 medium onion, chopped
1 c. sugar

½ c. plus 2 Tbsp. vinegar
½ c. oil
1 tsp. salt
1 tsp. celery salt

Combine veggies in a large bowl with a lid. Combine remaining ingredients in a small saucepan and stir. Cook until salt and sugar dissolve. Pour over cabbage mixture. Toss gently. Cover and chill at least 8 hours before serving. Will keep for several days in the refrigerator. Slaw will decrease in volume after marinating.

Beth Major

CORN AND TOMATO SALAD

½ c. fresh flat parsley,
   chopped
½ c. sour cream
½ c. mayonnaise
⅓ c. apple cider vinegar
1 ½ tsp. kosher salt
1 ½ tsp. dried oregano

1 tsp. pepper
1 ¾ c. grape tomatoes, halved
3 (12 oz.) pkg. frozen white
   Shoe Peg corn, thawed
1 green bell pepper, diced
½ c. red onion

Stir together first 7 ingredients in a large bowl. Add tomatoes and remaining ingredients, stirring well. Serve with slotted spoon.

Emily Jobe

CORN SALAD

2 cans (15 oz. each) whole
   kernel corn, drained
2 c. grated Cheddar cheese
1 c. mayonnaise
1 c. green bell pepper,
   chopped

½ c. red onion, chopped
1 (10.5 oz.) bag coarsely
   crushed chili-cheese corn
   chips

Mix first 5 ingredients and chill. Stir in corn chips just before serving.

Wanda Roach
Honorary Member

$\mathscr{K}$IM ADAMS' FRITO SALAD

1 can corn, drained
1 purple/red onion, sliced
   thin
1 red bell pepper, diced
1 green bell pepper, diced
1 yellow bell pepper, diced

2 c. Cheddar cheese,
   shredded
1 bag chili flavored Fritos
   corn chips
1 c. mayo

Mix and serve immediately. If you want to take it somewhere, it is recommended that you stir the Fritos chili flavored corn chips in when arriving, or it will be soggy.

Cookbook Committee

$\mathscr{G}$EORGIA'S LOADED POTATO SALAD

1 (5 lb.) bag red potatoes
2 c. grated Cheddar cheese
16 oz. carton sour cream
4 green onions or ½ medium
   size Vidalia onion, chopped
   (in season)

4.3 oz. pkg. real bacon pieces
1 tsp. black pepper
½ tsp. salt
½ c. Blue Plate mayonnaise

Scrub and quarter the potatoes. The larger ones you will need to cut into 6 pieces in order to keep the pieces about the same size. Boil the potatoes until fork-tender, not mushy, approximately 10 minutes. Drain the potatoes and let them cool in the colander while you assemble the remaining ingredients (about 5 minutes).

Clean and chop the onions and place in the pot you cooked the potatoes in; add 1 ¾ cups of the cheese, sour cream, mayonnaise, salt, pepper and bacon. Add the hot potatoes back to the pot and stir until blended. Transfer into a large serving bowl and sprinkle with the remaining ¼ cup of cheese.

Emilie Steele

$\mathscr{N}$EW POTATO SALAD

8 new potatoes, boiled
1 ½ c. Hellmann's
   mayonnaise
1 c. sour cream
1 ½ tsp. horseradish

1 tsp. celery seed
½ tsp. salt
1 c. dried parsley
1 medium chopped onion

Mix all but potatoes and onions and parsley together. Layer potatoes, mayo mixture, onions and parsley, ending with onions and parsley. Refrigerate at least one day before serving to let the flavors develop.

JoAnne Knieriem

GREEK ORZO PASTA SALAD

1 lb. orzo pasta, cooked and cooled*
1 container grape tomatoes, halved
1 cucumber, peeled and diced**
1 can black olives, drained and halved
½ (8 oz.) jar pepperoncini peppers, seeded and sliced into rings***
3 Tbsp. capers (optional, but adds a nice salty bite)
1 (4 oz.) container Feta cheese
1 Good Seasons Italian vinaigrette, made to directions on packet

*Do not overcook the pasta; otherwise it will be soggy. Take off 1 minute before instructions. You can substitute whole-wheat pasta.
**Recommend an English cucumber. If you use, you don't have to peel and adds great color.
***Can substitute banana peppers; both are spicy so use to taste.
Put cooked pasta in a bowl. Add ingredients one at at time. Adjust amounts to your taste. Add Feta next to last, again adjusting to your taste. Toss everything together and add vinaigrette a little at a time, stirring in between. Do not dump the entire vinaigrette on it; it will ruin it. I usually use about a quarter or so of vinaigrette. If possible, allow to sit in the refrigerator for half an hour for ingredients to cool and flavors to marry!

Renee Cavan

JULIA HOPE'S PASTA SALAD

1 lb. seashell pasta
¼ lb. Genoa salami, chopped
¼ lb. pepperoni, chopped
½ lb. Asiago cheese, grated
2 Tbsp. Parmesan cheese, grated
1 red bell pepper, diced
1 green bell pepper, diced
1 small can diced black olives
1 pt. cherry tomatoes, halved
1 pkg. dry Italian style salad dressing mix
¾ c. olive oil
¼ c. balsamic vinegar
½ Tbsp. dried oregano
½ Tbsp. dried parsley

Cook pasta according to package directions. Drain and cool under cold water. Combine cooked pasta with salami, pepperoni, cheeses, bell peppers, olives and tomatoes. Mix well; then cover and refrigerate.
Combine salad dressing mix, oil, vinegar, oregano and parsley in a jar with a lid. Shake well and refrigerate. Pour salad dressing mixture over pasta salad and stir well about an hour before serving. Promptly refrigerate any leftovers.

Jodi Sears

TRICOLOR PASTA SALAD

1 box tricolor pasta noodles,
  cooked and cooled
1 can artichoke hearts,
  drained and chopped (not
  marinated)
1 can chickpeas, drained
  and rinsed
1 small can diced tomatoes,
  drained and rinsed
1 small can sliced black
  olives

8 oz. Mozzarella or Provolone
  cheese cubes or shreds
bottle of Zesty Italian
  dressing
garlic powder to taste (a
  good bit, approximately 1 ½
  tsp.)
chives, basil, oregano,
  parsley to taste

Toss ingredients together and add dressing to coat. Allow to marinate overnight for best flavor, adding additional dressing as pasta absorbs it. This dish keeps well and actually gets better with time.

Anita Geoghagan
Honorary Member

HOMEMADE SPAGHETTI SAUCE

1 ½ lb. ground beef
1 large onion, chopped
1 clove garlic, chopped
1 (6 oz.) can tomato paste
1 (8 oz.) can tomato sauce
1 (14 ½ oz.) can stewed
  tomatoes

1 c. water
1 Tbsp. Italian seasoning
1 Tbsp. Worcestershire sauce
2 Tbsp. sugar
1 tsp. salt

Brown the ground beef and drain; then add onion and garlic. Sauté for about 5 minutes until the onion is tender. Add tomato paste, tomato sauce, stewed tomatoes, water and seasonings. Simmer for about 30 minutes.

Emily Jobe

YOUR FAVORITE RECIPES

Meats
& main dishes

Meat Cooking Chart

Roasting	Weight	Minutes Per lb.	Oven Temp.	Internal Temp.
FRESH PORK				
Rib and loin	3-7 lb.	30-40	325 F	175 F
Leg	5 lb.	25-30	325 F	170 F
Picnic shoulder	5-10 lb.	40	325 F	175 F
Shoulder, butt	3-10 lb.	40-50	325 F	170 F
Boned and rolled				
Shoulder	3-6 lb.	60	325 F	170 F
BEEF				
Standing ribs - rare	3-7 lb.	25	325 F	135 F
- medium	3-7 lb.	30	325 F	165 F
- well done	3-7 lb.	35	325 F	170 F
For rolled and boned roasts, increase cooking time 5 to 12 minutes.				
LAMB				
Shoulder- well done	4-10 lb.	40	325 F	190 F
Shoulder - boned and rolled	3-6 lb.	40	325 F	182 F
Leg- medium	5-10 lb.	40	325 F	175 F
Leg - well done	3-6 lb.	40-50	325 F	182 F
Crown - well done	3-6 lb.	40-50	325 F	182 F
SMOKED PORK				
Shoulder and picnic hams	5 lb.	30-40	325 F	170 F
	8 lb.	30-40	325 F	175 F
Boneless butt	2 lb.	40	325 F	180 F
	4 lb.	25	325 F	170 F
Ham	12-20 lb.	16-18	325 F	170 F
	Under 10 lb.	20	325 F	175 F
	Half Hams	25	325 F	170 F
VEAL				
Loin	4-6 lb.	35	325 F	175 F
Leg	5-10 lb.	35	325 F	175 F
Boneless shoulder	4-10 lb.	45	325 F	175 F
POULTRY				
Chicken	3-5 lb.	40	325 F	170 F
Stuffed	over 5 lb.	30	325 F	170 F
Turkey	8-10 lb.	20	325 F	175 F
	18-20 lb.	14	325 F	175 F
Duck	5-10 lb.	30	325 F	175 F

MEATS & MAIN DISHES

$\mathcal{B}$REAKFAST CASSEROLE

1 lb. bulk pork sausage (hot
  or mild)
1 (8 oz.) pkg. refrigerated
  crescent dinner rolls
2 c. Cheddar cheese,
  shredded

4 eggs, beaten
¾ c. milk
¼ tsp. salt
⅛ tsp. pepper

Preheat oven to 425°. Crumble sausage in skillet and cook over medium heat until browned. Drain well. Line the bottom of a greased 13 x 9 x 2 glass baking dish with crescent rolls, firmly pressing together perforations to seal. Sprinkle dough with browned sausage and top with shredded cheese. In a separate bowl, beat together eggs, milk, salt and pepper. Pour wet ingredients over cheese. Bake at 425° for 15 minutes or until set. Let stand 5 minutes before serving.

Millie Cline

$\mathcal{B}$RIE AND SAUSAGE BREAKFAST CASSEROLE

1 (8 oz.) Brie round (can
  substitute 8 oz. shredded
  Swiss cheese)
1 lb. ground hot pork
  sausage
6 white sandwich bread
  slices
1 c. grated Parmesan cheese
6 large eggs, divided

2 ½ c. whipping cream,
  divided
2 c. fat-free milk
1 Tbsp. chopped fresh sage or
  1 tsp. dried
1 tsp. seasoned salt
1 tsp. dry mustard
Garnishes: chopped green
  onions, shaved Parmesan
  cheese

Trim rind from Brie and discard; cut cheese into cubes and set aside. Cook sausage in a large skillet over medium-high heat, stirring until it crumbles and is no longer pink; drain well. Cut crusts from bread slices and place crusts evenly in bottom of a lightly greased 9 x 13 baking dish. Layer evenly with bread slices, sausage, Brie and Parmesan cheese. Whisk together 5 eggs, 2 cups whipping cream, milk and next 3 ingredients; pour evenly over cheeses. Cover and chill mixture for 8 hours.

Whisk together remaining egg and ½ cup of whipping cream; pour evenly over chilled mixture. Bake at 350° for 1 hour or until casserole is set. Garnish if desired.

Mary Johnston
Honorary Member

$\mathcal{S}$AVORY AND SIMPLE BREAKFAST FAVORITE

8 slices white or wheat
  bread, crust removed and
  cubed
1 lb. pork sausage, cooked, or
  8 oz. ham, chopped

4+ c. shredded sharp cheese
  (amount to your liking)
10 to 12 eggs, beaten
3 ½ c. milk
1 stick melted margarine

Remove crust from bread and cut in cubes. Place in greased (sprayed) 9 x 13 DEEP baking dish. Cook sausage until brown, stirring to crumble; drain well. If using ham, cut into small cubes. Spoon meat over bread cubes. Sprinkle cheese evenly over meat. Combine eggs and milk. Pour mixture over casserole. Pour melted margarine on top. Cover and refrigerate overnight.

Bake at 350° for 50 minutes to 1 hour, until brown and set. Often I use a disposable pan with HIGH sides.

Beth Cornelison

GRANNY RICKMAN'S BREAKFAST PIZZA

1 lb. sausage
1 can crescent rolls
1 c. shredded Cheddar cheese
1 c. Mozzarella cheese

1 c. American cheese
6 eggs
½ c. skim milk
1 tsp. oregano

Crumble sausage in skillet and cook until done; drain. Unroll crescent rolls in greased pan and pinch seams together. Crumble drained sausage over the crust evenly. Mix cheeses and sprinkle over sausage. Beat eggs, milk, salt, pepper and oregano; pour over cheese. Bake at 350° for 30 to 35 minutes.

Beth Major

MAKE AHEAD EGGS BENEDICT CASSEROLE

4 English muffins, split and
  toasted
8 slices Canadian bacon
¼ c. margarine
¼ c. flour
1 tsp. paprika
⅛ tsp. ground nutmeg

dash of fresh ground pepper
2 c. milk
2 c. shredded Swiss cheese
½ c. dry white wine or white
  Zinfandel
½ c. crushed cornflakes

In 9 x 13 x 2 baking dish, arrange muffins. Place bacon slices on each muffin. Half fill 10-inch skillet with water; bring just to simmer. Break egg into a dish. Carefully slide egg into water. Simmer until set. Remove eggs with slotted spoon, placing on top of each muffin stack.

For sauce, in a medium saucepan, melt margarine. Stir in flour, paprika, nutmeg and pepper. Add milk. Cook and stir until thickened and bubbly. Stir in cheese until melted. Stir in wine. Carefully spoon sauce over muffin stacks. Sprinkle cornflakes over muffin stacks. Cover; chill overnight.

To serve, bake, uncovered, in a 375° oven for 20 to 25 minutes.

JoAnne Knieriem

STUFFED CROISSANT FRENCH TOAST

6 large baked croissants
12 oz. cream cheese, softened
¼ c. peach nectar
¼ tsp. nutmeg

¼ tsp. ginger
½ c. light brown sugar
1 ½ c. chopped frozen
   peaches, drained

French Toast Batter:

4 eggs
¼ c. half and half
¼ tsp. salt
½ tsp. sugar

½ tsp. vanilla extract
1 tsp. ground cinnamon
¼ tsp. ground nutmeg

Slice the croissants open and set aside; let them get dried out. In a bowl, with a hand mixer, combine cream cheese, nectar, spices and sugar. Mix about 1 minute but be careful not to make mixture fluffy. Fold in peaches. Put in the refrigerator for a few hours or until set.

Fill croissants equally with cream cheese mixture. Refrigerate until ready to cook.

Melt 4 tablespoons butter in a skillet. Dip filled croissants in French toast batter. Over medium heat, place croissant in the skillet and lightly press down. Cook until toasty and brown. Flip and repeat. Serve warm.

Lisa Woodruff

CREME BRULEE FRENCH TOAST

½ c. butter
1 c. packed brown sugar
2 Tbsp. real maple syrup
6 (1-inch thick) sliced pieces
  French bread

4 eggs
1 ½ c. half and half
1 tsp. vanilla extract

Melt butter in saucepan over medium heat. Add brown sugar and syrup and stir until combined well. Pour into a 13 x 9 baking dish. Arrange French bread slices in single layer on top of butter mixture in pan. Whisk together eggs, half and half and vanilla. Pour over bread slices. Cover and chill overnight.

Remove dish and bring to room temperature. Bake in 350° oven for 20 minutes. Remove from oven and carefully flip individual pieces of bread over. Return to oven for 20 minutes or until lightly browned.

Jodi Sears

MORNING BRUNCH DELIGHT

(Makes its own syrup.)

1 c. brown sugar, packed
½ c. butter or 1 stick
2 c. corn syrup
1 loaf French bread, crust
   removed, sliced ¾-inch
   thick

8 eggs
2 c. milk
1 tsp. vanilla
Garnish: powdered sugar

Melt together brown sugar, butter and corn syrup in a saucepan over low heat; pour into a sprayed or greased 13 x 9-inch baking pan. Arrange bread slices over mixture and set aside. Mix eggs, milk and vanilla with a whisk; pour over bread, coating all slices. Cover and refrigerate overnight.

Uncover and bake at 350° for 30 minutes or until light brown. Sprinkle with powdered sugar.

Delicious served with fresh blueberries, strawberries and raspberries. (Often I have increased the amount of milk and eggs to make more custard-like.)

Beth Cornelison

BACON CHEESE QUICHE

1 (9-inch) deep pie shell
1 c. grated Swiss cheese
3 eggs, beaten
½ c. Parmesan cheese, grated

½ lb. bacon, fried and
   crumbled
1 (3 oz.) pkg. cream cheese,
   cut into ½-inch cubes
1 ½ c. whipping cream

Preheat oven to 350°. Place shell on cookie sheet and place the grated Swiss cheese on the bottom of the crust. Place the crumbled bacon on the Swiss cheese. Mix the eggs, cream and Parmesan cheese together and pour over the Swiss cheese/bacon. Place ½-inch cheese cubes on top of the egg mixture. Bake at 350° for 45 minutes.

Julie Pennington

$\mathcal{Q}$UICHE

2 c. grated Monterey Jack cheese	¼ c. meat (ham bits or crumbled bacon)
2 c. grated Swiss cheese	¼ c. broccoli or spinach, chopped in small pieces
2 extra large eggs	1 small onion, chopped and blended with mixed ingredients
¾ c. light cream	
1 Tbsp. flour	
salt and pepper to taste	
8 oz. mushrooms, chopped	1 (9-inch) unbaked pie shell

Mix together cheeses in a bowl. In a blender, combine eggs, light cream, flour and salt and pepper. Starting and ending with cheese mixture, arrange alternate layers of cheese and extra ingredients in the pie shell. Then pour blender mixture over the top. Bake at 350° for 1 hour or until light brown on top (a knife inserted should come out clean). Freezes well uncooked.

JoAnne Knieriem

$\mathcal{B}$ACON CHICKEN WRAP

1 to 2 lb. chicken tenderloins	1 can cream of chicken soup
½ lb. bacon	1 c. sour cream

Preheat oven to 325°. Spray a 9 x 13 pan. Wrap each chicken tenderloin in a piece of bacon and place in the pan. Mix the soup and sour cream together and pour over top of the chicken/bacon mixture. Cover with foil and bake for 2 hours. After 2 hours, increase the temperature to 350°. Remove foil and bake for 14 minutes.

Julie Pennington

$\mathcal{C}$HICKEN A LA KING

½ c. onion, chopped	1 to 1 ⅓ c. light cream (half and half)
¼ c. green bell pepper, chopped	1 lb. chicken, boiled and cubed
¼ c. butter or margarine	
2 cans cream of mushroom soup (undiluted)	a dash of red pepper
	6 English muffins

Sauté onion and green pepper in butter until tender. Blend in soup and light cream, stirring until smooth. Add chicken. Stir over medium heat until hot. Sprinkle red pepper on top. Spoon over English muffins that have been split, buttered and broiled.

I like to serve this entree with saffron rice and steamed asparagus or broccoli.

Wendy Landry

CHICKEN AND CHEESE

4 chicken breasts, cooked
  and chopped/shredded
1 (8 oz.) carton sour cream
1 can cream of chicken soup

1 sleeve buttery crackers,
  crushed
1 stick butter, melted

Preheat oven to 350° and grease an 8 x 8 baking dish. Cook and chop/shred chicken and spread in bottom of baking dish. Mix the sour cream and soup; spread over the chicken. Add the crushed crackers and spread with melted butter over the crackers. Bake for 30 minutes or until bubbly in the center.

Julie Pennington

CHICKEN BUNDLES

4 oz. cream cheese, softened
1 (13 oz.) can chicken
1 Tbsp. sesame seeds
¼ tsp. parsley

2 cans crescent rolls
1 Tbsp. finely chopped onion
  or dried onion
1 egg, beaten

Combine all ingredients and mix well. Take crescent rolls and divide into 2 triangles together forming 8 rectangles. Pinch seams closed and pat each one into bigger squares. Place a spoonful of chicken mixture in the center, layering the roll like flower petals so that the roll is sealed. Brush the tips with 1 beaten egg and top with sesame seeds and parsley. Bake at 375° for 15 to 20 minutes or until golden brown.

Lori Davis

CHICKEN CASSEROLE

4 chicken breasts, cooked
  and diced (reserve broth)
3 c. chicken broth
1 (10 oz.) can cream of
  chicken soup
1 (10 oz.) can cream of
  mushroom soup

1 (15 oz.) can Niblets corn,
  drained
1 (15 oz.) can English peas,
  drained
1 (8 oz.) pkg. cornbread
  stuffing mix

Combine chicken, broth, soups and vegetables. Pour into greased 2-quart baking dish. Top with stuffing mixture. Bake for 30 minutes or until browned.

Robyn McEntyre

CHICKEN MARSALA

1 lb. skinless, boneless chicken breasts	1 c. fresh mushrooms
2 chicken bouillon cubes	1 egg, beaten
1 c. Marsala wine	2 Tbsp. olive oil
	flour

Trim fat from chicken. Dip in egg, then flour. Brown both sides of chicken breast in skillet with olive oil. Add bouillon cubes and wine. Cover with mushrooms. Simmer for 20 minutes.

Melissa Auringer

CHICKEN POT PIE

4 c. Pepperidge Farm stuffing (any type you like)	½ c. melted butter
	6 slices bread, crumbled

Mix ingredients together. Preheat oven to 375°. Press the mixture into greased 9 x 13 pan; reserve approximately 1 cup.

1 can cream of chicken soup	2 (10 oz.) bags frozen veggies
1 can cream of celery soup	2 Tbsp. minced onion
1 ½ c. milk	dash of pepper
3 c. cooked chicken	

In saucepan heat ingredients. Pour over the dressing mix. Top with remaining stuffing mix. Bake at 375° for 30 to 40 minutes.

Julie Pennington

ROBYN'S CHICKEN POT PIE

1 chicken, boiled and deboned (reserve broth)	1 (15 oz.) can Veg-All, drained
1 (10 oz.) can cream of chicken soup	1 stick butter, melted
½ can water	1 ½ c. self-rising flour
	1 ½ c. buttermilk
	2 c. chicken broth

Do not stir! Place chicken on bottom of 9 x 13 pan. Pour Veg-All over chicken. In separate bowl, mix water and soup; then pour over chicken and Veg-All. Mix butter, flour and buttermilk together and pour on top. Pour 2 cups broth on top of everything. Bake at 350° for 1 hour.

Robyn McEntyre

CHICKEN POT PIE CASSEROLE

4 to 6 boneless, skinless
  chicken breasts
1 (10 oz.) can cream of
  chicken soup
1 can peas and carrots
  mixture, drained
2 c. chicken broth
salt and pepper to taste
1 ½ c. self-rising flour
1 c. milk
2 Tbsp. margarine, melted

Boil chicken until tender. Reserve 2 cups broth. Chop or shred chicken and place in greased 9 x 13-inch casserole dish. Spread soup and vegetable mixture over chicken; pour broth over mixture. Sprinkle with salt and pepper. Mix flour, milk and margarine. Pour over chicken mixture. Bake at 350° for 50 minutes or until crust looks done.

Melissa Whatley

CHICKEN ROLLS

1 can cream of mushroom
  soup
½ c. milk
1 c. Cheddar cheese, grated
1 (8 oz.) pkg. crescent rolls
2 to 3 large skinless and
  boneless chicken breasts,
  cooked and chopped

Preheat oven to 350°. Heat soup, cheese and milk in pan or microwave until cheese is melted. Separate rolls and place approximately 1 tablespoon of chicken at large end of roll and roll up. Place in casserole dish and pour cheese sauce over rolls. Bake 30 minutes until rolls rise and brown. Serve immediately.

Mary Johnston
Honorary Member

CHICKEN ROLL-UPS

2 (8 oz.) cans reduced fat
crescent dinner rolls
1 (10 ¾ oz.) can 98% fat-free
cream of chicken soup
(undiluted)

¾ c. grated Cheddar cheese
or Swiss cheese (or any
cheese of choice)
½ c. milk

Filling:

4 oz. cream cheese (very soft;
I used ⅓ less fat cream
cheese)
2 Tbsp. butter (very soft but
not melted)
½ to 1 tsp. garlic powder
1 tsp. minced onion flakes
2 large cooked chicken
breasts, finely chopped (or
use about 2 c.; can use
cooked turkey)

½ to ¾ c. finely grated
Cheddar cheese
½ tsp. seasoned salt
½ tsp. ground black pepper
or to taste
2 Tbsp. milk
1 to 2 c. grated Cheddar
cheese (for topping)

Set oven to 350°F. Spray a 9 x 13 dish with cooking spray. Mix together milk, ¾ cup cheese and undiluted chicken soup (can season with black pepper if desired).

For the Filling: (Make certain that the cream cheese and butter are very soft.) In a bowl, mix the soft cream cheese with butter until very smooth; then add in garlic powder. Add in the chopped chicken, onion and Cheddar cheese; mix well until combined. Add in 2 tablespoons milk; mix to combine (add in a little more if the mixture seems too dry). Season with seasoned salt or white and black pepper to taste.

Unroll the crescent rolls. Place 1 heaping tablespoon chicken mixture (or a little more) on top of each crescent triangle; then roll up starting at the thicker end. Drizzle a small amount of soup mixture on the bottom of the dish. Then place the crescent rolls seam side down on top of the creamed mixture in the casserole.

Drizzle the remaining sauce on top (you don't have to use the full amount of cream sauce; just use as much as desired) and sprinkle with 1 cup (or more) grated cheese, or amount desired. Bake for about 30 minutes.

Julie Pennington

CHICKEN STUFFED SHELLS

1 (12 oz.) box pasta shells, cooked
4 chicken breasts, cooked and chopped
1 (10 ¾ oz.) can cream of chicken soup
1 (10 ¾ oz.) can cream of mushroom soup

1 c. sour cream
1 c. shredded Mozzarella cheese
1 Tbsp. chicken broth
1 Tbsp. lemon juice
1 tsp. garlic powder

Topping:
2 Tbsp. melted butter
¼ c. bread crumbs

¼ c. grated Parmesan cheese

Preheat oven to 350°. Prepare shells according to package directions. Remove from water and place on a towel to drain.

To make filling: combine all remaining ingredients in a medium bowl. Mix well. Stuff each shell with the chicken mixture and place in a 13 x 9 inch baking dish.

Mix topping ingredients together and sprinkle over stuffed shells. Bake 30 minutes or until bubbly.

Andrea Payne
Honorary Member

CHICKEN, BISCUITS AND MUSHROOM GRAVY

1 Tbsp. olive oil
8 oz. sliced button mushrooms
1 medium yellow onion, diced
2 cloves garlic, minced
¼ c. white wine

1 c. half and half
salt and black pepper to taste
1 rotisserie chicken
fresh baked biscuits, canned or homemade

Remove chicken meat from bone, shred and keep warm. Cook the biscuits according to package directions or family recipe.

In a large skillet over medium-high, heat the oil. Add the mushrooms, onion and garlic; then sauté until the mushrooms are browned and the pan is nearly dry, about 5 minutes. Add the wine and stir to deglaze the pan. When the wine has evaporated, stir in the half and half; then bring to a simmer. Season with salt and pepper; set aside.

Place one biscuit on each serving plate. Top with a heap of warmed, shredded chicken; then spoon ample amounts of mushroom gravy over it.

Anita Geoghagan
Honorary Member

CROCK-POT CHICKEN AND DUMPLINGS

4 skinless, boneless chicken
  breasts, halved
2 Tbsp. butter
2 cans condensed cream of
  chicken soup

1 onion, finely chopped
2 cans refrigerated biscuit
  dough, torn into pieces

Place chicken, butter, soup and onion in slow cooker; fill with enough water to cover. Cover and cook on high for 5 to 6 hours. About 30 minutes before serving, place torn biscuit dough in slow cooker (poke holes in dough before adding to pot). Cook until dough is no longer raw in the center. Serve and enjoy!

Lori Davis

DOT'S CHICKEN SPAGHETTI

3 lb. chicken breasts
4 Tbsp. salad oil
2 beef bouillon cubes
2 tsp. salt
¼ tsp. pepper
¼ c. minced onion
¼ c. minced bell pepper
1 tsp. paprika

½ c. chopped pimento
12 oz. thin spaghetti
1 c. ripe olives, sliced
1 small can mushroom pieces
½ c. water chestnuts, sliced
2 c. grated processed
  Cheddar cheese

Wash and dry chicken. Brown in hot fat or oil in skillet. Place in deep soup pot. Add bouillon cubes and just cover with boiling water. Add salt and pepper. Cover; simmer until very tender, at least 3 hours.

Pull meat from bones and cut into small pieces. Skim fat from broth. Add enough water to make 2 quarts. In skillet where chicken was browned, lightly brown onion and green pepper with paprika. Add to broth. Add pimento and chicken. Heat to boiling; add spaghetti and cook uncovered until tender. DO NOT DRAIN. Add olives, chestnuts and mushrooms. Add 1 cup cheese. Heat until very hot. Place on platter; sprinkle with rest of cheese.

Mary Johnston
Honorary Member

EASY CROCK-POT CHICKEN AND NOODLES

4 boneless, skinless chicken
  breasts
2 cans cream of chicken soup

½ c. butter, sliced
42 oz. chicken broth
1 bag egg noodles

Put all ingredients, except noodles, into the crock-pot. Cover and cook on low for 8 hours. Add bag of egg noodles and cook 1 more hour.

Kelly Brannam

ENCHILADA CASSEROLE

2 chickens or 5 skinless,
  boneless chicken breasts,
  cooked and deboned
1 onion, chopped fine
2 cans chopped green chilies
½ stick butter or margarine
1 can cream of mushroom
  soup
1 can cream of chicken soup
1 large can evaporated milk
½ c. broth
approximately 24 corn
  tortillas
2 c. grated cheese (Monterey
  Jack or Mexican mixture is
  best)
paprika to taste

Sauté onion and chilies in butter or margarine just until onions are translucent. Add soups and milk to onion mixture. Simmer on low 10 minutes. Meanwhile, soak corn tortillas in broth. Grease a 13 x 9-inch deep pan with cooking spray or butter. Line pan with corn tortillas that have been soaked in broth (approximately 4 to 6 tortillas per layer). Layer sauce, chicken and grated cheese, then tortillas again until all gone. Sprinkle top with layer of cheese and paprika (if desired).

Casserole freezes well at this point. When ready to eat, bake at 325° for 45 minutes.

Bonny Spears

FAMILY FAVORITE CHICKEN

½ c. dry Italian seasoned
  bread crumbs
½ c. grated Parmesan cheese
4 tsp. dried parsley
½ tsp. salt
⅛ tsp. pepper
6 boneless, skinless chicken
  breast halves
¼ c. milk
½ c. butter (1 stick), melted
2 small garlic cloves,
  crushed
juice of 1 lemon

Combine the bread crumbs, Parmesan cheese, parsley, salt and pepper in a shallow dish and mix well. Dip each chicken breast in the milk and dredge in the bread crumb mixture. Arrange in a greased 9 x 13-inch baking dish. Combine butter, garlic and lemon juice in a bowl and mix well. Drizzle over chicken. Bake at 350° for 40 minutes or until done.

Susan Ikerd

FOUR CHEESE CHICKEN FETTUCCINE

8 oz. fettuccine noodles
1 can cream of mushroom
  soup
1 (8 oz.) cream cheese, cubed
1 (4.5 oz.) jar sliced
  mushrooms, drained
1 c. whipping cream

½ c. butter
¼ tsp. garlic powder
¾ c. Parmesan cheese, grated
  or shredded
½ c. shredded Mozzarella
  cheese and Swiss cheese
2 ½ c. cubed chicken, cooked

Topping:
⅓ c. bread crumbs
2 Tbsp. melted butter

2 Tbsp. Parmesan cheese

Cook fettuccine according to package directions. Meanwhile, in a saucepan combine the soup, cream cheese, mushrooms, whipping cream, butter and garlic powder. Cook and stir over medium heat until blended. Reduce heat to low, add cheese and stir until melted. Add chicken and heat through. Drain fettuccine and add to chicken mixture. Transfer to a sprayed baking dish.

Combine topping ingredients and sprinkle over chicken mixture. Cover with foil. Bake at 350° for 30 minutes. Uncover and bake 5 to 10 more minutes.

Kim Fowler

GLORIFIED CHICKEN

1 ½ lb. boneless, skinless
  chicken breast
1 can cream of chicken soup
1 (16 oz.) carton sour cream
1 stick margarine, melted

1 sleeve Ritz crackers,
  crushed
1 Tbsp. poppy seed
onion salt to taste
salt and pepper to taste

Boil chicken with salt, pepper and onion salt. Cut chicken into chunks. Combine soup and sour cream; stir in chicken. Place in 8-inch square baking dish. Mix together margarine, crackers and poppy seed. Sprinkle on top of chicken. Bake at 350° approximately 30 minutes or until browned and bubbly.

Kim Fowler

HERBED MUSTARD CHICKEN

1 frying chicken, cut into pieces (remove as much skin as possible)	½ tsp. basil, minced
	½ tsp. fresh ground pepper
	2 dashes of cayenne
¼ c. olive oil	½ c. dry white wine
4 cloves garlic, pressed	6 Tbsp. vinegar (apple or white)
½ c. onion, diced	
½ tsp. thyme leaves	¼ c. spicy brown mustard
½ tsp. oregano, minced	1 Tbsp. honey

Mix first 8 ingredients except chicken (through cayenne) in a glass bowl. Cover with paper towel and microwave on High until warm, about 45 seconds. Combine remaining ingredients in glass bowl and stir thoroughly. Add to first mixture. Put chicken pieces in glass pan and pour marinade over chicken, coating thoroughly. Cover pan with clear plastic and pre-cook chicken in microwave on Medium setting, turning frequently until nearly cooked through (about 15 minutes on mid-range power setting). Put in refrigerator overnight or 6 to 8 hours minimum.

Drain chicken pieces and grill on low heat setting until golden brown, basting frequently. To increase servings, multiply all ingredients by number of chickens used.

JoAnne Knieriem

HONEY LIME CHICKEN ENCHILADAS

1/3 c. honey
1/4 c. lime juice (about 2 large limes)
2 tsp. to 1 Tbsp. chili powder
2 large cloves garlic, finely minced or 1/2 tsp. garlic powder
1 lb. boneless, skinless chicken breasts (about 2 large breasts), cooked and shredded

12 corn tortillas
2 c. Mexican cheese blend, shredded (1 small bag usually is 2 c.)
1 (14 oz.) can green enchilada sauce (mild or medium, to your taste)
1/2 to 3/4 c. heavy cream
nonstick cooking spray
1 Tbsp. chopped cilantro (to garnish)

Preheat oven to 350°F. Place the cooked and shredded chicken in a medium sized bowl. Set aside. In a small bowl, place the honey, lime juice, chili powder and minced garlic or garlic powder. Whisk together thoroughly to combine. Pour this mixture over the chicken and cover with plastic wrap. Allow to marinate while you prepare the tortillas, 30 minutes or up to 1 hour, in the refrigerator.

Heat a large griddle until a drop of water skitters across (about 350°F). Spray the surface with nonstick cooking spray or oil it with a little bit of canola oil in between each round of tortillas. Heat tortillas about 20 seconds on each side until warm and flexible and some golden brown spots have appeared. Remove the tortillas from the griddle and keep them between a couple of paper towels until ready to use.

Spray the sides and bottom of a 9 x 13-inch baking dish lightly with cooking spray. In a medium bowl combine the enchilada sauce and the heavy cream. Spread about 1/2 cup of the mixture in the bottom of the oiled baking dish. Add a large spoonful (about 2 tablespoons) of the chicken mixture to the center of each tortilla in a line. Cover the chicken with a large tablespoon (or big pinch) of cheese; then roll the tortilla up from one side to make a rolled enchilada. It will be more of an overlap on the seam side than rolled tightly.

Place the enchilada seam side down in the baking dish starting at one end with the long edge parallel to the longest side of the pan so that you end up with two columns of six enchiladas each. Repeat with the remaining chicken, cheese and tortillas. You will use about 1 1/2 cups of the cheese for the filling; set the remainder aside for topping the enchiladas in the pan. Add the remaining marinade mixture to the enchilada sauce and cream mixture, if desired. Pour this mixture over the top of all the enchiladas. Sprinkle with the remaining cheese. Bake the enchiladas for 30 to 35 minutes, until the cheese is melted and bubbly and starting to brown on top.

Jennifer Stanley

$\mathcal{H}$OT CHICKEN SALAD

2 to 3 c. cooked and chopped
  chicken
1 c. finely chopped celery
1 small bell pepper
2 Tbsp. finely chopped onion
½ c. pimento, diced
1 c. grated cheese

2 Tbsp. lemon juice
1 c. mayonnaise
1 can cream of chicken soup
1 small pkg. potato chips,
  crumbled
1 small can garden peas,
  drained

Mix all ingredients, saving a small amount of chips to crumble on top. Bake in oven 25 minutes at 350°.

Judy McGarity
Honorary Member

$\mathcal{K}$IM ADAMS' FIREHOUSE CHICKEN

1 ½ lb. chicken (breast or
  tenderloin strips)
1 c. buttermilk
2 to 3 c. all-purpose flour
½ tsp. garlic

½ tsp. onion powder
½ tsp. salt
½ tsp. pepper
4 to 5 c. vegetable oil

Soak chicken in buttermilk for 1 to 2 hours. Blend flour, garlic powder, onion powder, salt and pepper together. Separate chicken and dredge in flour. Place vegetable oil into a 12-inch skillet or deep fryer. Heat oil to approximately 375° and cook chicken for 5 to 7 minutes or until golden brown.

Cookbook Committee

$\mathcal{K}$ING RANCH CHICKEN CASSEROLE

1 large onion, chopped
1 large green bell pepper,
  chopped
1 (10 oz.) can diced tomato
  and green chiles
2 c. chopped cooked chicken
1 tsp. chili powder
1 (10 ¾ oz.) can cream of
  chicken soup (undiluted)

1 (10 ¾ oz.) can cream of
  mushroom soup (undiluted)
¼ tsp. salt
¼ tsp. garlic powder
¼ tsp. pepper
2 c. (8 oz.) shredded Cheddar
  cheese, divided
12 (6-inch) flour or corn
  tortillas or tortilla chips or
  Doritos

Mix onions, green peppers, chicken, soups, canned tomatoes and spices. Tear tortillas into 1-inch pieces. Layer in a 13 x 9 lightly greased dish: ⅓ of tortilla pieces, ⅓ of chicken mixture and ⅔ cup cheese. Repeat 2 more times. Bake at 350° for 30 to 35 minutes.
Note: Freeze casserole up to 1 month, if desired. Thaw in refrigerator overnight and bake as directed.

Robyn McEntyre

LEMON CHICKEN

1 lb. boneless, skinless chicken breasts	1 egg, beaten
2 chicken bouillon cubes	flour
1 c. white cooking wine	1 Tbsp. olive oil
1 lemon	cooked rice

Trim fat from chicken. Dip chicken in egg, then flour. Brown chicken breast in skillet with olive oil. Add bouillon cubes and wine. Slice lemon and place on top of chicken. Simmer 20 minutes. Serve over rice.

If you like more lemon flavor, squeeze the juice of another lemon in the pan while simmering.

Melissa Auringer

LILLIAN THOMASON'S CHICKEN IN WINE

1 whole chicken, cut into pieces	1 c. (or less) ripe black olives, chopped
1 stick margarine	1 small jar pimentos, chopped
½ green pepper, chopped	
½ c. chopped onion	1 c. cooking sherry or any white wine
½ c. chopped celery	
salt, pepper, sugar to taste	1 c. chicken stock
1 clove garlic, finely minced	1 medium can mushrooms (stems and pieces)

Skin chicken and pat dry. Melt butter on low heat and brown chicken on both sides. Lay browned chicken aside. Sauté green pepper, onions, celery and garlic in margarine. Add ripe olives, mushrooms and pimento, cooking sherry or wine and chicken stock. Bring all ingredients to a boil and add salt and pepper to taste. Add about 1 teaspoon of sugar to bring out the flavors.

Put chicken in baking dish, pour sauce over, cover and cook about 1 hour in oven at 350°. May also be cooked in covered skillet on top of stove over low heat.

Carolyn Weaver
Honorary Member

$\mathcal{S}$IMPLE PARMESAN CHICKEN

½ c. Italian seasoned
    breadcrumbs or panko
½ c. grated Parmesan cheese
½ tsp. salt
¼ tsp. pepper

6 boneless, skinless chicken
    breasts, thinly sliced
¼ c. milk
½ c. butter, melted
½ Tbsp. garlic salt
2 Tbsp. lemon juice

Combine breadcrumbs, Parmesan cheese, salt and pepper. Dip each chicken breast in milk and then into the breadcrumb mixture. Place in a greased 9 x 13 baking dish. Combine butter, garlic salt and lemon juice in a bowl and drizzle over the chicken. Bake at 350° for 40 minutes or until done.

Jamie Bobo
Honorary Member

$\mathcal{S}$TOG'S CHICKEN TETRAZZINI

4 to 5 boneless chicken
    breasts
1 box spaghetti or angel hair
    pasta
1 can cream of mushroom
    soup

1 can Cheddar soup
½ c. shredded Cheddar
    cheese
½ c. milk

Boil chicken about 20 minutes. Remove from heat, let cool and cut into bite size pieces.

Preheat oven to 350°. Cook pasta according to package directions and using same pot as chicken if desired. Add remaining ingredients to pot and slowly cook until you have a rich, creamy sauce. Layer a casserole dish with the cooked pasta, top with chicken and then pour sauce over chicken. Additional shredded cheese can also be added at this time. Bake about 15 minutes.

Stores well in fridge, and leftovers are awesome!

Marcy Stogner

WHITE CHICKEN ENCHILADAS

10 soft taco shells
2 c. cooked, shredded chicken
2 c. shredded Monterey Jack
  cheese
3 Tbsp. butter

3 Tbsp. flour
2 c. chicken broth
1 c. sour cream
1 (4 oz.) can diced green
  chilies

Preheat oven to 350°. Grease a 9 x 13 pan. Mix chicken and 1 cup cheese. Roll up in tortillas and place in pan.

In a saucepan, melt butter; stir in flour and cook 1 minute. Add broth and whisk until smooth. Heat mixture over medium heat until thick and bubbly. Stir in sour cream and chilies. Do not bring to boil as it will curdle the sour cream. Pour over enchiladas and top with remaining cheese. Bake 22 minutes and then place under high broiler for 3 minutes to brown cheese. Watch carefully.

Julie Pennington

KIM ADAMS' SMOKED TURKEY QUESADILLAS AND DIP

4 flour tortillas (10-inch)
1 c. grated Pepper Jack
  cheese
8 to 10 slices smoked turkey

2 Tbsp. butter
1 c. sour cream
1 Tbsp. chili powder
juice of 1 lime

Sprinkle each tortilla with ¼ cup of cheese and then place 2 to 3 slices of smoked turkey over on one side. Fold tortilla in half. Place 1 ½ teaspoons of butter in 12-inch nonstick skillet over medium heat. Then place folded prepared tortilla in pan and cook until golden brown on both sides (approximately 2 to 3 minutes). Cut into wedges. Dip in a mixture of sour cream, chili powder and lime juice to taste.

Cookbook Committee

QUAIL IN A CHAFING DISH

8 quail
salt and pepper to taste
½ c. butter
3 oz. sherry

juice of 1 ½ lemons
4 Tbsp. Worcestershire sauce
2 Tbsp. all-purpose flour
1 c. cream

Split birds or leave whole. Season to taste. Brown birds, breast side down, lightly in butter in a Dutch oven. Add enough water to keep birds from burning. Cover; cook for about 1 hour. When almost done, add sherry, lemon juice and Worcestershire. Cook about 20 minutes longer; remove birds.

Combine flour and cream; add to gravy, stirring until thickened. Put birds and gravy in a chafing dish. Let stand until ready to serve. Light chafing dish to reheat about ½ hour before serving. Doves are also delicious cooked this way.

Linda Hasty
Honorary Member

BACON WRAPPED PORK TENDERLOIN

1 c. brown sugar
6 Tbsp. salt
2 Tbsp. chili powder
1 tsp. black pepper
1 tsp. Old Bay seasoning

1 tsp. ground chipotle pepper
1 tsp. paprika
2 pork tenderloins
1 lb. bacon (10 to 11 strips)

In a mixing bowl combine spices, making sure all ingredients are combined well. Trim any unwanted fat or silver skin away from the tenderloin. Apply a liberal amount of rub mixture to the top, sides and bottom of the tenderloin. On a cutting board or work surface lay out bacon and create a basket weave of bacon. Place the weave of bacon on top of the tenderloin and wrap any extra bacon under the bottom of the tenderloin.

Preheat a smoker to 225°. Place the tenderloin in the smoker until the internal temperature of the tenderloin reaches a minimum of 165° (approximately 2.5 hours). (If you do not have a smoker, you can cook in an oven at same temperature for approximately 2.5 hours.)

Charlee Renfro

$\mathcal{B}$ARBECUE PULLED PORK SANDWICHES

pork butt (approximately 2 ½
  lb.)
1 can Diet Pepsi

½ bottle Sweet Baby Ray's
  barbecue sauce
Lawry's seasoned salt

Generously coat pork butt with seasoned salt; don't be afraid to cover it all. Place in a crock-pot and pour in soda and barbecue sauce. Cover and cook on low for 4 to 5 hours or until butt reaches 145°. After 4 hours or so, take two forks and shred meat into bite size chunks. Let it sit in juice to soak up the flavor. It can stay warm in crock-pot while serving and can easily be reheated the next day. Serve on a kaiser roll and add more barbecue sauce if needed or desired.

Julie Pennington

$\mathcal{C}$ROCK-POT HERB PORK ROAST

4 large garlic cloves,
  quartered
1 pork loin roast (boneless;
  about 4 to 5 lb.)
1 tsp. salt
1 scant tsp. dried leaf thyme
½ tsp. dried leaf sage,
  crumbled
¼ tsp. dried leaf rosemary,
  crumbled

¼ tsp. dried tarragon,
  crumbled (optional)
dash of ground cloves or
  allspice
1 tsp. grated lemon peel
  (optional)
½ c. water
3 Tbsp. cornstarch (optional)
3 Tbsp. water (optional)

Cut 16 small pockets into roast and insert garlic slices. In a small bowl combine salt, herbs and lemon peel. Rub seasoning mixture into the roast. Pour ½ cup water into slow cooker; add the roast. Cover and cook on low for 8 to 10 hours. Pork roast should read at least 145° on an instant-read thermometer. Serves 8.

If desired, thicken juices. Remove roast from juices. Combine cornstarch with the 3 tablespoons water, stir until smooth and then stir into the crock-pot juices. Cook on high until thickened. Serve with the pork roast.

Melissa Whatley

$\mathscr{K}$IM ADAMS' RED BEANS AND RICE

2 Tbsp. vegetable oil
1 medium onion, chopped
1 (4 oz.) can green chilies
1 lb. smoked sausage
1 (14 ½ oz.) can dark red
   kidney beans

8 oz. block Monterey Jack
   cheese, shredded
1 c. uncooked rice
butter
Tabasco sauce

In a 3-quart saucepan place vegetable oil, chopped onion, green chilies and smoked sausage (cut into bite size pieces) over medium heat. Sauté until onions are translucent. While this is cooking prepare rice by placing 2 cups of water and 1 teaspoon butter into a saucepan; bring this to a boil and then add 1 cup uncooked rice. Simmer on low for 20 minutes. When rice is complete, add rice to 3-quart saucepan, along with the kidney beans. Mix thoroughly. When serving, add ¼ cup shredded cheese to red beans and rice along with 2 or 3 shakes of Tabasco sauce.

Cookbook Committee

$\mathscr{L}$ILLIAN THOMASON'S ITALIAN LOAF SANDWICH

1 lb. bulk sausage
½ c. chopped green pepper
1 (½ oz.) spaghetti sauce mix
   packet

1 can diced tomatoes
1 loaf French bread

Brown sausage and green pepper together in large skillet; drain. Stir spaghetti sauce packet and tomatoes into sausage mixture.

Cut top off French bread loaf; set aside. Hollow inside and crumble into small pieces. Reserve 1 ½ cups of crumbled bread and mix with sauce mixture. Simmer 10 minutes. Using a large spoon, fill hollowed loaf. Sprinkle with grated Mozzarella cheese on top of filled bread and place top on the loaf. Wrap in foil and heat 20 to 30 minutes at 350°. Remove from oven; let sit 5 minutes. Unwrap and slice.

Beth Allison
Honorary Member

STUFFED PORK TENDERLOIN

1 (6 oz.) pkg. long grain wild
   rice mix
½ c. boiling water
½ c. dried apricots, chopped
2 green onions, finely
   chopped
½ c. fresh mushrooms,
   chopped
¼ c. green pepper, chopped
2 Tbsp. butter
3 Tbsp. pecans, chopped

1 Tbsp. fresh parsley,
   chopped
$\frac{1}{8}$ tsp. salt
$\frac{1}{8}$ tsp. pepper
dash of cayenne pepper
dash of garlic powder
4 (1 ½ lb.) boneless pork
   tenderloins
4 slices bacon
canned apricot halves
fresh parsley

Cook rice according to package directions; set aside. Pour boiling water over apricots; let stand 20 minutes to soften; drain. Sauté green onions, mushrooms and green pepper in butter until tender. Add rice, apricots, pecans, parsley and seasonings. Stir until combined. Cut a lengthwise slit on top of each tenderloin, being careful not to cut through bottom and sides. Spoon half of stuffing into the opening of one tenderloin; place second tenderloin over it. Tie together securely with string. Place on rack in roasting pan with 2 bacon slices on top. Repeat with remaining tenderloins. Place aluminum foil tent over tenderloins. Bake at 325° for 1 hour 30 minutes to 2 hours or until meat thermometer registers 170°. Remove foil the last 30 to 40 minutes. Remove from oven. Let stand 5 minutes. Remove string. Slice. Garnish with apricot halves and parsley.

Linda Hasty
Honorary Member

BAKED ZITI

1 lb. lean ground beef
1 c. onions, chopped
1 Tbsp. olive oil
1 tsp. pepper
pinch of salt
32 oz. can meatless sauce

1 c. chicken broth
16 oz. pkg. ziti pasta, cooked
   and drained
2 c. Mozzarella cheese,
   shredded
1 c. Parmesan cheese, grated

Preheat oven to 350°. In a large skillet, heat oil and cook onions for 8 minutes. Add beef and cook until no longer pink (drain excess fat). Stir in sauce, chicken broth, pepper and salt.

Stir 1 cup of sauce into the cooked ziti pasta. Place ½ of the ziti into a 13 x 9 baking dish. Place ½ cup of Mozzarella cheese and ½ cup Parmesan cheese. Top with the rest of the sauce. Top with the rest of the pasta. Cover and bake for 20 minutes. Sprinkle with remaining Mozzarella cheese and Parmesan cheese. Cook until golden brown.

Laura Stanley

BEEF IN WINE SAUCE

1 lb. stew beef
2 Tbsp. dry onion soup mix
1 can cream of mushroom
  soup

2 Tbsp. dry red wine
1 Tbsp. Minute tapioca

Mix all ingredients together and refrigerate overnight covered. Cook in crock-pot on lowest setting 8 hours. Serve over rice!

Susan Ikerd

BEEF AND POTATO BOATS

4 large baking potatoes
4 slices bacon
¾ lb. ground beef
1 onion, chopped, or 1 Tbsp.
  onion salt

1 ½ tsp. salt
½ c. sour cream
2 Tbsp. butter
¼ c. milk
¼ c. American cheese, grated

Bake potatoes at 400° for 45 minutes to 1 hour. Set aside. Cook bacon; drain and crumble. Mix beef and onions; shape into patties. Brown in a skillet for 5 minutes on each side. Break up into small chunks. Add salt, sour cream and bacon; set aside.

Split potatoes; scoop out. Combine with milk and butter; mash until smooth. Put beef in potato shell. Put mashed potatoes on top. Sprinkle with cheese. Bake at 400° for 20 minutes.

Judy McGarity
Honorary Member

BEEF STROGANOFF

2 onions, chopped
3 Tbsp. butter
2 Tbsp. flour
1 c. beef stock or consommé
1 Tbsp. tomato paste or
  ketchup
1 tsp. Worcestershire sauce

½ tsp. salt
⅛ tsp. pepper
1 ½ lb. sirloin, cut in thin
  strips
½ lb. mushrooms
1 c. sour cream

Sauté onions in butter until yellow. Stir in flour and then gradually add other liquids. Cook and stir until smooth and thickened. In hot frying pan, sauté beef strips until brown. Add beef to sauce and salt and pepper. Sauté mushrooms in frying pan, adding additional butter if needed. Add mushrooms to meat and sauce. Just before serving, add sour cream and heat. Do not let boil.

This is a good dish to make the day ahead. Always add sour cream just before reheating.

Wanda Roach
Honorary Member

SPAGHETTI CASSEROLE

2 (30 oz.) jars Ragu Chunky
  Tomato, Garlic and Onion
  spaghetti sauce
1 (16 oz.) box spaghetti,
  cooked according to pkg.
  directions

approximately 2 ½ lb. ground
  beef, cooked and drained
2 c. double pizza cheese (a
  blend of cheeses)

Heat spaghetti sauce with cooked beef. Add a little margarine to cooked, drained noodles and toss. Mix the noodles and meat sauce together. Place in a 9 x 13 disposable pan and sprinkle cheese on top. Bake at 250° for 30 minutes or until cheese melts.

This is a great casserole for family and friends in need of a meal. Freezes well. If frozen, thaw in fridge and adjust baking time accordingly.

Cookbook Committee

COOK'S DELIGHT

1 ½ lb. ground beef
1 large can tomato sauce
1 (8 oz.) pkg. cream cheese
1 (8 oz.) container sour
  cream

1 medium onion, chopped
½ box vermicelli pasta
oregano (optional)
Cheddar cheese (optional)

Cook vermicelli according to directions on box; drain and place in bottom of greased casserole. Brown meat; add onion while browning. Add tomato sauce to browned meat mixture and simmer 2 to 3 minutes. Cream together softened cream cheese and sour cream. Spread over pasta. Pour meat and tomato sauce mixture over cheese and pasta. Bake at 350° for 30 minutes. A little oregano can be added to the meat sauce or some Cheddar cheese on top for variety.

Mary Johnston
Honorary Member

CROCK-POT ROAST

pot roast of your choice and
  size
1 pkg. Ranch dressing mix
  (powdered)

1 pkg. Italian dressing mix
  (powdered)
1 pkg. brown gravy mix
  (powdered)
½ c. water

Place roast in crock-pot. Mix the packets together with water. Pour over the crock-pot and cook on low for 6 hours.

Julie Pennington

$\mathcal{E}$ASY ROAST BEEF

3 to 5 lb. beef roast (any
   inexpensive cut will work)
4 oz. pkg. Lipton onion soup
   mix
14 oz. jar yellow
   pepperoncini peppers

10 oz. can low sodium
   chicken broth
10 oz. can low sodium beef
   broth
sliced Provolone cheese
   (optional)

Place beef roast in crock-pot. Pour onion soup mix, beef and chicken broths over roast. Cut tops and stems off each pepperoncini pepper and return them to their original jar in the juice. Pour entire jar of pepperoncini peppers with juice over beef roast and mix with large spoon to blend soups. Cover. Cook on low for 11 hours.

Note: Eleven hours, not 8 hours like most recipes! This is important to the success of this roast.

The last ½ hour of cooking time, take roast out of crock-pot and "shred" the meat apart with a knife or fork and return meat to the juices in crock-pot for 30 minutes. Serve on your favorite bun or hoagie roll, with extra juice on the side. Serving Suggestion: Place Provolone cheese slice over the sandwich and microwave for 35 seconds before serving; then spoon additional au jus over the bread!

Jennifer Stanley

$\mathcal{F}$RENCH DIP SANDWICHES

2 to 3 lb. chuck roast, cut
   into cubes
2 cans beef broth
1 pkg. au jus gravy (dry in
   pkg.)

1 pkg. Good Seasons Zesty
   Italian salad dressing (dry
   in pkg.)
water to cover meat

Cook in a crock-pot overnight on low. Serve on French or Italian sub style buns/rolls.

Cheryl Young
Honorary Member

ITALIAN PIE

1 (10 oz.) box frozen chopped
  spinach
1 ¼ lb. ground meatloaf
  blend (beef/pork)
1 tsp. dried Italian seasoning
¼ c. diced pimientos, drained
¼ c. pepperoni

1 (13.75 oz.) jar bruschetta
  spread
2 eggs, beaten
2 c. shredded Italian blend
  cheese
1 ready to bake rolled pie
  crust

Place spinach in colander under cool running water to thaw; break into smaller pieces if possible. Preheat oven to 425°F.

Preheat large sauté pan on medium-high 2 to 3 minutes. Add ground meat and Italian seasoning; brown 5 to 7 minutes, stirring to crumble meat, or until no pink remains. Drain spinach thoroughly by pressing firmly against colander. Stir pimientos, pepperoni, spinach and bruschetta spread into meat; cook 1 to 2 minutes or until thoroughly heated.

Transfer to a medium bowl and set aside 1 to 2 minutes to cool. Stir in eggs and cheese; transfer to a 9 x 13-inch baking dish. Unroll pie crust over meat mixture. (Stretch dough to fit or use extra dough that overlaps sides to cover extra space at each end of the baking dish; press edges together on each end.) Trim and seal or crimp edges. Cut two small slits in center of crust. Bake 20 to 30 minutes or until mixture is bubbly and crust is golden. Serve.

Barbara Manous
Honorary Member

LILLIAN THOMASON'S SWISS STEAK

1 lb. sirloin steak
1 small onion, chopped
1 bell pepper, chopped
1 can tomato soup

1 Tbsp. brown sugar
1 tsp. Worcestershire sauce
salt and pepper to taste

Flour pieces of sirloin steak and brown in oil. Remove steak from pan and place in greased casserole dish. Mix remaining ingredients in a bowl and pour over steak. Cover with foil and bake at 350° for 1 hour or until tender.

Beth Allison
Honorary Member

$\mathcal{L}$ILLIE MAE BROWNLEE'S ZUCCHINI CASSEROLE

1 ½ lb. hamburger meat
4 to 5 medium zucchini
  squash, sliced
2 to 3 onions
1 green bell pepper

2 cans stewed tomatoes (one
  Mexican style and the other
  Italian style)
oregano to taste
salt and pepper to taste
1 c. shredded sharp Cheddar

Brown hamburger meat in an electric skillet. Drain off oil. Add zucchini, onions, bell pepper, stewed tomatoes and seasoning. Let cook 45 minutes. Sprinkle cheese over the top and let melt.

Mary Johnston
Honorary Member

$\mathcal{M}$EXICAN CASSEROLE

1 lb. ground beef
1 small onion, diced
1 packet taco seasoning
1 can kidney beans, drained

1 can Ro-Tel tomatoes
Cheddar cheese, grated
flour tortillas

Brown beef and drain. Add onion, taco seasoning, beans and Ro-Tel tomatoes. Let simmer. In a baking dish, layer tortillas, beef mixture and then cheese until all is used. Bake at 350° until cheese is melted and casserole is hot and bubbly.

Ashley Rusbridge

$\mathcal{M}$IMI JO'S BEEF STROGANOFF

1 pkg. stew meat
1 sweet onion, chopped
1 can mushrooms (optional)
1 can beef stock
16 oz. container sour cream

garlic salt to taste
butter
flour
rice

Cut stew meat into small pieces; flour and season meat with garlic salt. Melt ½ stick butter in deep-dish frying pan. Add onion to butter; cook until translucent. Add floured meat to pan; brown. Add beef stock, cover and cook 20 minutes, stirring occasionally. Add sour cream and mushrooms. Simmer 5 to 10 minutes. Serve over cooked rice.

Karen McClellan
Honorary Member

$\mathcal{N}$O PEEK BEEF CASSEROLE

2 lb. all meat stew beef or round steak, cut into bite size pieces	1 (4.5 oz.) can or jar sliced mushrooms (undrained)
1 packet dry onion soup mix	1 (10 ¾ oz.) can cream of mushroom soup (undiluted)

Mix all ingredients in a 2-quart casserole dish and cover tightly. Bake at 300° for 3 hours. Serve over noodles or yellow rice. DO NOT PEEK while cooking!

Kim Fowler

$\mathcal{S}$COTT'S ZITI RECIPE

1 (16 oz.) pkg. dry ziti pasta	6 oz. sliced Provolone cheese
1 lb. lean ground beef	6 oz. sliced Mozzarella cheese
1 onion, chopped fine	1 ½ c. sour cream
2 (28 oz.) jars spaghetti sauce (Hunt's canned four cheese variety)	½ c. grated Parmesan cheese
	¼ c. chopped fresh basil

Bring a large pot of lightly salted water to a boil. Add pasta and cook for 8 to 10 minutes or until al dente; drain. Put a small amount of olive oil or butter in the noodles to keep them from sticking. In a large skillet, brown beef over medium heat. Add onions; sauté until tender. Drain off fat and add spaghetti sauce; simmer for about 15 minutes.

Preheat oven to 350°F (175°C). In a lightly greased deep 9 x 13 baking dish, place about half of the pasta; top with a layer of Provolone and Mozzarella cheese slices. Spread on a layer of half the spaghetti sauce mixture and the sour cream. Cover with remaining pasta, cheese, sauce and sour cream. Sprinkle a layer of Parmesan cheese and fresh basil on top.

Note: Freezes well at this step. If frozen, thaw in refrigerator overnight; then proceed to next step just before eating. Otherwise, bake in preheated oven for about 30 minutes or until cheese and sauce are bubbly.

Bonny Spears

SOUTHWEST BEEF AND BLACK BEAN ENCHILADAS

1 (17 oz.) fully cooked beef
  pot roast
1 (8 oz.) can tomato sauce
⅔ c. salsa verde
6 (10-inch) flour tortillas

8 oz. shredded Monterey Jack
  cheese, divided
1 (15 oz.) can black beans,
  drained and rinsed
2 Tbsp. chopped green
  chilies, divided

Preheat oven to 400°. Microwave pot roast on High 2 to 3 minutes or until warm. Transfer gravy (from pot roast) to medium saucepan. Finely shred meat using two forks; place in medium bowl.

Stir tomato sauce and salsa verde into gravy; cook on medium setting for 3 to 4 minutes or until hot. Add ¾ cup of the gravy mixture to pot roast. Spread ½ cup gravy mixture over bottom of 9 x 13-inch baking dish.

Spoon down center of each tortilla: ⅓ cup beef mixture, ¼ cup cheese, 3 tablespoons black beans and 1 teaspoon chilies. Roll tortillas around filling and place, seam side down, in baking dish. Top enchiladas with remaining ¾ cup gravy mixture and ½ cup cheese. Bake 18 to 20 minutes or until cheese melts and enchiladas have browned slightly.

Serve with fiesta rice. Sour cream, salsa and lettuce make great toppings!

Cindy Prien

SPAGHETTI BAKE

1 (15.5 oz.) can diced tomatoes with garlic and olive oil	1 ½ tsp. Italian seasoning
	1 ½ tsp. seasoned salt
	1 ½ tsp. sugar
2 (8 oz.) cans tomato sauce	2 small bay leaves
1 c. water	1 ½ lb. ground beef
½ c. onion, diced	8 oz. uncooked angel hair pasta
2 cloves garlic, chopped	
¼ c. chopped fresh parsley leaves	1 c. sharp Cheddar, grated
	1 c. Monterey Jack, grated

In a stockpot, combine the canned tomatoes, canned tomato sauce, water, onions, peppers, garlic, parsley, seasoning, sugar and bay leaves. Bring to a boil over medium-high heat. Reduce heat and let simmer, covered, for about an hour. Remove bay leaves.

While that is simmering, crumble the ground beef in a large skillet. Cook over medium-high heat until no pink color remains. Drain the fat from the meat. Add the ground beef to the stockpot. Simmer for 20 more minutes. Cook the pasta according to the package directions.

Preheat the oven to 350°F. Cover the bottom of a deep 13 x 9-inch pan with sauce. Add a layer of pasta and then a little less than ½ of each cheese; repeat the layers, ending with the sauce.

If taking to someone, this freezes well at this point, or to eat now bake in the oven for 30 minutes. Top the casserole with the remaining cheese, return it to the oven and continue to cook until the cheese is melted and bubbly, about 5 more minutes. Cut into squares before serving.

Bonny Spears

SUPER MEAT LOAF

2 lb. lean ground beef	1 Tbsp. Worcestershire sauce
1 lb. ground pork sausage	1 tsp. yellow mustard
18 saltine crackers, crushed	½ c. firmly packed brown sugar, divided
1 onion, finely chopped	
2 large eggs, lightly beaten	½ to ¾ c. ketchup

Preheat oven to 350°. Combine first 7 ingredients and ¼ cup brown sugar in a medium bowl just until blended. Place in a lightly greased 13 x 9-inch baking dish and shape mixture into a 10 x 5-inch loaf. Bake at 350° for 1 hour.

Remove from oven and drain. Stir together remaining ¼ cup brown sugar and ketchup; pour over meat loaf. Bake 15 more minutes or until meat thermometer inserted into thickest portion registers 160°. Remove from oven; let stand 20 minutes. Remove from baking dish before slicing.

Anita Geoghagan
Honorary Member

BARBECUE SHRIMP

1 ½ lb. Georgia wild
  harvested large shrimp,
  peeled, deveined and tails
  off
3 slices bacon, cut into bite
  sized pieces
½ lb. butter
2 Tbsp. Dijon mustard

1 ½ tsp. chili powder
¼ tsp. basil
¼ tsp. thyme
1 tsp. black pepper
½ tsp. oregano
2 cloves minced garlic
2 Tbsp. crab boil seasoning
½ tsp. Tabasco sauce

Preheat oven to 350°. In an ovenproof skillet, fry bacon until lightly browned. Leave bacon grease in pan. Add all other ingredients to the pan, except shrimp. Simmer 5 minutes. Toss shrimp into sauce and cook for 12 minutes uncovered in preheated oven at 350°.

Serve shrimp and sauce over yellow rice, accompanied by French bread and tossed green salad.

Patti Skelton
Honorary Member

BLACKENED FISH WITH MANGO SALSA

1 ripe mango (1 c.), cubed
½ c. fresh cilantro, chopped
¼ c. chopped red onion
1 jalapeno pepper, minced
2 Tbsp. fresh lime juice

2 to 4 skinless fish fillets
  (depending upon size)
1 Tbsp. melted butter
2 Tbsp. prepared blackened
  or jerk seasoning

Combine mango and next 4 ingredients in a bowl. Cover and chill until ready to serve. Brush fish with melted butter and coat both sides with seasoning. Heat a large cast-iron or heavy bottom skillet until hot. Cook fish 2 minutes on each side or until opaque. Serve with mango salsa.

If cooking multiple fish pieces: Sear the outside but do not cook through. Place on a lightly greased baking sheet. Cover and set aside until ready to serve. If waiting more than 30 minutes, place in refrigerator. Finish by baking at 400° for 5 to 7 minutes, or until fish is opaque and flakes easily with a fork.

Anita Geoghagan
Honorary Member

JACKSON'S SALMON

1 lb. fresh salmon fillets with
   skin removed
1 Tbsp. butter
¼ c. 100% real maple syrup

¼ c. teriyaki sauce or
   marinade
1 tsp. diced garlic

Melt butter in nonstick pan over medium heat. Add fresh salmon fillets to the pan and cook for 3 to 5 minutes. While salmon is cooking, whisk together 100% real maple syrup, teriyaki sauce and diced garlic. Carefully turn salmon over and spoon sauce over each fillet. Continue to cook 3 to 5 more minutes or until fish flakes easily with a fork. Spoon warm sauce from the pan over each fillet as it is served.

Jodi Sears

PIERSON'S SHRIMP SCAMPI

1 stick butter
1 ½ Tbsp. diced garlic
1 heaping Tbsp. chopped
   fresh parsley

1 Tbsp. lemon juice
2 lb. fresh or frozen shrimp,
   shelled, deveined, with
   tails removed

Melt butter in nonstick pan over medium heat. Once butter is melted, add diced garlic, chopped parsley and lemon juice to the pan. Stir for 3 minutes until well combined. Add shrimp to the pan and stir well until all shrimp is coated in butter mixture. Continue to cook over medium heat for 5 to 7 minutes or until shrimp turn pink.

Jodi Sears

MUSHROOM PASTA

8 oz. bow tie pasta
2 Tbsp. unsalted butter
16 oz. presliced portabella
   mushrooms
2 Tbsp. minced garlic

1 tsp. salt
⅔ c. Marsala wine or
   creamed sherry
1 c. heavy cream

Fill a large saucepan with water and bring to a boil. Add pasta and boil for 9 to 10 minutes or until tender. Melt butter in a large sauté pan. Add mushrooms and garlic; cook for 5 to 6 minutes, stirring occasionally, or until mushrooms soften and begin to release their juices. Season with salt and add wine. Cook 5 minutes, stirring occasionally. Add cream. Cook 3 to 4 minutes, stirring occasionally or until sauce has reduced by about one third. Drain pasta and stir into sauce.

Wanda Roach
Honorary Member

TORTILLA PIZZA

1 (7-inch) whole-wheat
  tortilla
¼ c. shredded low-fat
  Mozzarella cheese

¼ tsp. Italian seasoning
1 sliced plum tomato
1 tsp. olive oil

On a nonstick pan place tortilla, top with cheese, sprinkle with Italian seasoning and drizzle with olive oil. Top with slices of tomato. Bake at 425° for 10 minutes or until tortilla is crisp.

Robyn McEntyre

YOUR FAVORITE RECIPES

Recipe

Page Number

MEATS & MAIN DISHES

Vegetables

How To Can Vegetables

POINTS ON PACKING

Raw pack. Pack cold raw vegetables (except corn, lima beans, and peas) tightly into container and cover with boiling water.

Hot pack. Preheat vegetables in water or steam. Cover with cooking liquid or boiling water. Cooking liquid is recommended for packing most vegetables because it may contain minerals and vitamins dissolved out of the food. Boiling water is recommended when cooking liquid is dark, gritty or strong-flavored, and when there isn't enough cooking liquid.

PROCESSING IN A PRESSURE CANNER

Use a steam-pressure canner for processing all vegetables except tomatoes and pickled vegetables.

Directions. Follow the manufacturer's directions for the canner you are using. Here are a few pointers on the use of any steam-pressure canner:

- Put 2 or 3 inches of boiling water in the bottom of the canner; the amount of water to use depends on the size and shape of the canner.
- Set filled glass jars or tin cans on rack in canner so that steam can flow around each container. If two layers of cans or jars are put in, stagger the second layer. Use a rack between layers of glass jars.
- Fasten canner cover securely so that no steam can escape except through vent (petcock or weighted-gage opening).
- Watch until steam pours steadily from vent. Let it escape for 10 minutes or more to drive all air from the canner. Then close petcock or put on weighted gage.
- Let pressure rise to 10 pounds (240 degrees F). The moment this pressure is reached, start counting processing time. Keep pressure constant by regulating heat under the canner. Do not lower pressure by opening petcock. Keep drafts from blowing on canner.
- When processing time is up, remove canner from heat immediately.

With glass jars, let canner stand until pressure is zero. Never try to rush the cooling by pouring cold water over the canner. When pressure registers zero, wait a minute or two, then slowly open petcock or take off weighted gage. Unfasten cover and tilt the far side up so steam escapes away from you. Take jars from canner.

HOW TO CHECK CANNING JARS

The first step in home canning should take place long before food and equipment are assembled and ready to go. Jars and other supplies should be checked prior to the canning session. In that way, you can replace damaged supplies and purchase new ones to avoid costly delays or inconvenience.

Here are some tips to help you.

Choosing mason jars. Jars manufactured especially for home canning generically are called mason jars and must be used when preserving. They are designed with a specially threaded mouth for proper sealing with mason lids. So, can with standard mason jars only.

Preparing glass jars. Check all jars, rings and lids carefully. Discard any with nicks or cracks in top sealing edge and threads that may prevent airtight seals. Rings should be free of dents or rust. Select the size of closures - widemouth or regular - that fits your jar. Wash jars in hot, soapy water and rinse well. Then place in boiling water for 10-15 minutes. Keep jars in hot water until ready to use. Boil lid according to package directions.

Closing glass jars. Always wipe jar rim clean after food product is packed. Place lid on jar with button side up. Screw rings on firmly, but don't force. Do not re-tighten rings after processing or cooling.

A new lid that snaps down and clicks as the jar cools, providing visible proof of sealing, called Magic Button® is made by Owens-Illinois. Its red button pops up when the seal is broken. The Magic Mason jars that go with the special lids have metric measurements as well as customary U.S. measurements molded on the side.

Jar transfer. Use jar lifter or long-handled canning tongs to transfer jars to and from canner safely. Place hot jars on rack or towel, allowing 2-inches of air space on all sides for jars to cool evenly.

VEGETABLES

ASPARAGUS PARMESAN

1 ½ lb. fresh asparagus
1 c. dry white wine
½ c. water
¼ c. melted butter or
   margarine

½ tsp. salt
¼ tsp. pepper
¼ c. Parmesan cheese

Thoroughly wash the fresh asparagus, cutting away all of the less tender parts of the stalks. Simmer asparagus (covered) in white wine and water until crisp but still tender (about 10 minutes). Drain and place the asparagus on platter and pour the melted butter over the asparagus. Next, sprinkle the asparagus with salt, pepper and Parmesan cheese. Place under the broiler for about 2 to 3 minutes.

April Turner

BARBEQUED BAKED BEANS

1 medium onion, chopped
1 lb. bacon, fried crisp
1 lb. ground beef
1 (15 oz.) can kidney beans,
   drained
2 (15 oz.) cans pork and
   beans

1 (15 oz.) can butter beans,
   drained
1 ½ c. ketchup
¾ c. white sugar
¾ c. brown sugar

Fry bacon, let cool and then break into pieces. Brown the ground beef and onions. Grease 2-quart dish and add ground beef, bacon and onions. Add the remaining ingredients and stir well. Bake at 350° for 1 hour.

Julie Pennington

$\mathcal{T}$HE BEST BAKED BEANS YOU'LL EVER EAT

1 lb. ground beef	*2 Tbsp. molasses*
2 large cans Bush's	*½ c. brown sugar*
traditional baked beans	*2 Tbsp. yellow mustard*

Brown and drain ground beef. In large casserole dish, mix beef with all other ingredients. Bake at 400° for 20 minutes.

Stephanie Bagwell

$\mathcal{B}$ROCCOLI AND RICE CASSEROLE

1 (10 oz.) box frozen chopped	*8 oz. block Velveeta cheese,*
broccoli	*cubed*
1 stick butter	*1 can cream of mushroom*
1 large onion, chopped	*soup*
	1 c. cooked rice

Cook broccoli in small amount of water; then drain (according to directions on box). In a pan, sauté onion in butter until the edges barely begin to caramelize. Add cheese to broccoli and stir on medium heat until cheese is melted. Add soup and onion mixture. Add rice. Stir just until ingredients are incorporated and put into a greased casserole dish. Bake at 350° for 30 minutes.

Molly Mercer

$\mathcal{B}$ROCCOLI CASSEROLE

2 (10 oz.) pkg. frozen chopped	*1 c. sharp Cheddar cheese,*
broccoli	*grated*
1 (10 ½ oz.) can cream of	*1 medium onion, chopped*
mushroom or cream of	*¼ c. mayonnaise*
broccoli soup	*3 eggs, beaten*

Cook broccoli in salted water until tender; drain. Mix well with remaining ingredients. Pour into greased 2-quart casserole dish. Bake at 350° for 45 minutes.

Melissa Whatley

$\mathscr{M}$OTHER'S BROCCOLI AND RICE CASSEROLE

1 (10 oz.) pkg. frozen chopped broccoli	1 ½ c. cooked rice (not instant)
½ c. butter or margarine	1 (8 oz.) jar Cheez Whiz
½ c. celery, chopped	1 (10 ¾ oz.) can cream of mushroom soup
½ c. onion, chopped	

Preheat oven to 350°. Cook broccoli according to package directions; drain. Melt butter; saute celery and onion until clear. Combine broccoli, vegetables, rice, cheese and mushroom soup; blend well. Pour into 2-quart baking dish. Bake at 350° for 20 minutes.

JoEllen Wilson
Honorary Member

$\mathscr{R}$OASTED CAULIFLOWER

2 Tbsp. olive oil	½ tsp. salt
1 head cauliflower	¼ tsp. pepper

Preheat oven to 425°. Drizzle a 15 x 10-inch jelly roll pan with 1 tablespoon olive oil. Cut cauliflower vertically into ¼-inch thick slices. Arrange in a single layer on prepared pan. Drizzle cauliflower with remaining olive oil; sprinkle with salt and pepper. Bake at 425° for 25 to 30 minutes or until golden brown. Sprinkle with salt to taste.

Anita Geoghagan
Honorary Member

$\mathscr{C}$ORN BAKE

1 box Jiffy corn muffin mix	1 c. sour cream
1 (16 oz.) can whole kernel corn, drained	1 stick butter, melted
1 (16 oz.) can cream-style corn	2 eggs

Heat oven to 350°. Grease 2-quart baking dish. Melt butter and set aside. Mix the two cans of corn together; stir in the eggs and then Jiffy corn muffin mix. Add the melted butter and stir until well mixed. Pour into the greased baking dish and bake for 45 minutes to 1 hour, or until center is set and no longer jiggles.

Julie Pennington

CORNBREAD CASSEROLE

12 oz. can Green Giant Fiesta corn, drained	1 egg
12 oz. can creamed corn	1 pkg. Jiffy corn muffin mix
8 oz. sour cream	1 small onion, chopped
	salt and pepper to taste

Preheat oven to 350°. Combine all ingredients in a bowl and mix well. Bake in a greased 8 x 8-inch casserole dish for 45 minutes or until done in the center.

Melissa Auringer

BUNDLE OF BEANS

4 (16 oz.) cans Italian-cut green beans	½ c. vinegar
1 small onion, chopped	1 tsp. dry mustard
1 c. brown sugar	1 tsp. seasoned salt
	4 slices bacon, cut in half

Drain beans, wash and put in 13 x 9 casserole dish. Place chopped onions on top of beans. Mix brown sugar, vinegar, dry mustard and salt. Pour over beans and onions (do not mix). Place sliced bacon on top of everything. Bake at 375° for 30 minutes uncovered. Bake at 350° for 30 minutes covered.

Beth Major

GREEN BEAN BUNDLES

2 cans whole green beans	½ tsp. garlic salt
½ lb. bacon, strips cut in half	sprinkle of salt, pepper and
⅓ box brown sugar	onion powder
1 stick butter or margarine	

Drain beans; season with salt, pepper and onion powder. Wrap 4 to 5 beans at a time in a half a piece of uncooked bacon and place in a 9 x 13-inch casserole dish. In saucepan, heat butter, brown sugar and garlic salt until the brown sugar dissolves. Pour over green beans. Bake at 350° for 20 minutes or until bacon is cooked.

Millie Cline

GREEN BEANS

1 large can cut green beans	4 Tbsp. olive oil
1 medium can cut green beans	⅛ c. sugar
	salt and pepper

Pour green beans into a medium saucepan. Add the remaining ingredients. Cook on high until water cooks down and turn to low. Add as much or little of salt and pepper as you want.

Kelley Hyde

$\mathcal{G}$RITS, SMOKED GOUDA, BACON AND CORN BAKE

10 slices bacon, chopped
2 c. frozen whole kernel corn,
  thawed and drained
4 c. low sodium chicken
  broth
1 ¼ c. quick cooking grits

½ c. heavy whipping cream
2 c. (18 oz.) shredded smoked
  Gouda cheese
½ c. minced green onion
2 large eggs
½ tsp. salt

Preheat oven to 350°. In a large skillet, cook bacon and corn over medium heat, stirring frequently, until bacon is crisp. Drain well and set aside. In a large saucepan, bring broth to a boil over medium-high heat. Slowly stir in grits; reduce heat and simmer for 4 to 5 minutes or until thickened. Stir in cream. Remove from heat.

Add cheese, green onion and bacon/corn mixture to grits. Add eggs and salt, stirring until combined. Spoon mixture into a greased 13 x 9 baking dish. Bake for 40 to 50 minutes or until golden brown. Let stand for approximately 10 minutes before serving.

Jamie Morgan
Honorary Member

$\mathcal{S}$PICY GRITS

3 cans chicken broth
4 Tbsp. butter
1 ⅓ c. quick cooking grits

1 (8 oz.) brick Velveeta
  cheese
2 (10 oz.) cans Ro-Tel
  tomatoes, drained

Preheat oven to 350°. Bring broth and butter to a boil in a large pot over medium heat. Add grits and cook for 5 minutes, stirring often, or until thick. Remove from heat and add cheese and stir until melted. Stir in Ro-Tel tomatoes and pour into a lightly greased 9 x 13 dish. Bake at 350° for 30 minutes. This dish can be made the day before and refrigerated.

Emily Jobe and Amanda Locke

$\mathcal{T}$OMATO GRITS

3 to 5 pieces bacon or real
  bacon bits
2 cans chicken broth

1 c. quick grits
1 can Ro-Tel
1 c. shredded Cheddar cheese

Cook bacon and put aside. Bring chicken broth to boil (add a little bit of bacon grease). Stir in grits and Ro-Tel. Simmer for 15 minutes or until done. Stir occasionally. Add cheese and bacon crumbles. Serve for breakfast or at dinner with shrimp.

Amy Graham

CAROLYN BEAVERS MACARONI DISH

1 lb. sharp cheese, grated
1 lb. elbow macaroni
½ c. onion, finely chopped
¼ c. pimento, finely chopped

1 can cream of mushroom
   soup
1 c. mayonnaise
2 Tbsp. butter
cheese crackers

Cook macaroni per package directions; remove from heat and drain just before done. Mix remaining ingredients with macaroni. Put crushed crackers over top. Cook 25 minutes in 300° oven. Freezes well.

Mary Johnston
Honorary Member

CREAMY MICROWAVE CHEESE AND MACARONI

16 oz. elbow macaroni,
   cooked as directed
16 oz. Velveeta cheese, cubed
4 c. shredded sharp cheese

3 (8 oz.) cans evaporated
   milk
2 Tbsp. margarine
2 Tbsp. self-rising flour
1 c. milk

Preheat oven to 400°. Spray a 2 ½-quart microwave dish; melt margarine. Stir in flour. Use a wire whisk to stir in evaporated milk. Cook on High in microwave for 5 minutes; remove and stir. Cook on High for 4 minutes; remove and stir. Repeat this 3 minute process until mixture is thick. For thickness or thinness, you can add up to 1 cup of milk. Add cubed Velveeta and shredded sharp cheese. Microwave 2 minutes; remove and stir. Repeat this process until smooth. Pour and stir in cooked macaroni. Bake at 400° about 30 minutes until bubbling. This recipe is easy to double for a large crowd.

Michelle L. Whitmire
Honorary Member

CROCK-POT MAC AND CHEESE

8 oz. macaroni
4 c. shredded sharp Cheddar
   cheese
1 c. whole milk

12 oz. evaporated milk
¼ c. butter, softened
2 eggs, beaten
¼ c. grated Parmesan cheese

Cook and drain macaroni. Mix cooked macaroni, 3 cups of shredded Cheddar cheese, whole milk, evaporated milk, butter and beaten eggs together in a large mixing bowl. Stir well. Pour mixture into crock-pot and sprinkle the top with remaining cup of shredded cheese and ¼ cup of Parmesan cheese. Cook on low setting for 3 to 4 hours depending on how fast your crock-pot cooks. DO NOT stir while cooking.

Lori Davis

$\mathcal{K}$AREN'S CHEESY MACARONI AND CHEESE

8 oz. box macaroni
1 c. grated sharp cheese
  (more if you like)
1 jar Kraft Old English
  cheese

3 cans (12 oz. each)
  evaporated milk
2 eggs

Cook macaroni until done, salting to taste. While macaroni is cooking, prepare the following. Mix milk and cheese in double boiler and gradually warm until cheese is melted. (You may need to mix with an electric or hand mixer to completely mix.) When mixture becomes melted and macaroni is almost ready, beat eggs in a bowl and stir in some of the cheese mixture. Add this to all of the cheese mixture and cook until it begins to thicken. Drain macaroni and add to the cheese mixture.

Pour into a buttered 9 x 13-inch casserole dish and sprinkle with grated cheese. Cook at 350° for about 20 minutes. Keep checking and remove from oven while the center of casserole is still "jiggly." You may prepare the night before, but if refrigerated, cooking time will be longer.

Barbara Manous
Honorary Member

$\mathcal{M}$ACARONI AND CHEESE

1 (8 oz.) pkg. elbow macaroni
2 c. milk
¼ c. all-purpose flour
1 tsp. onion salt

2 (10 oz.) blocks sharp
  Cheddar cheese, shredded
1 c. soft bread crumbs
¼ c. butter, melted

Cook and drain macaroni. Mix milk, flour and onion salt in Mason jar. Cover and shake vigorously for 1 minute. Stir together flour mixture, 3 ½ cups cheese and macaroni. Pour into lightly greased 13 x 9 pan and top with remaining cheese and bread crumbs and drizzle with melted butter. Bake at 350° for 45 minutes.

Jodi Sears

THREE CHEESE MACARONI AND CHEESE

2 c. Cheddar cheese, grated	4 eggs
2 c. Colby Jack cheese, grated	3 c. milk
	1 c. heavy cream
2 c. shredded Velveeta	½ stick butter, melted
1 box elbow macaroni	salt and pepper to taste

Preheat oven to 350°. In a saucepan, bring noodles to a boil until they are just undercooked. Drain noodles. In a bowl, mix eggs, milk, heavy cream and salt and pepper. Pour half of mixture into a greased 9 x 13 pan. Add a layer of noodles on top.

In a separate bowl, combine Cheddar, Colby Jack and Velveeta cheeses. Top noodles with ½ the three cheese mixture. Repeat the layers. Poke holes in the layers and pour butter on top. Cover with foil tightly and bake for 45 minutes. Remove foil and bake for an additional 10 minutes. Let stand for 10 to 15 minutes before serving.

Laura Stanley

MARINATED VIDALIA ONIONS

4 big Vidalia onions	½ c. Hellmann's mayonnaise
2 c. water	celery
1 c. sugar	salt
½ c. white vinegar	

Slice and separate rings of onions. Bring water, sugar and vinegar to boil. Remove from heat. Add onions. Pour into glass bowl and marinate overnight in refrigerator.

Next day, drain onions thoroughly. Add mayonnaise and celery. Salt to taste. Mix well; serve chilled or at room temperature.

JoAnne Knieriem

ONION PIE

Crust:

1 ½ c. Ritz crackers, crushed ½ c. butter

Filling:

3 ½ c. sliced onions
½ c. butter
1 c. milk
2 eggs, slightly beaten

1 tsp. salt
½ lb. sharp Cheddar cheese,
    grated

Crust: Melt the butter and add the crushed crackers. Press into bottom of a 10-inch pie plate.

Filling: Cook the onions and butter until tender; do not brown. Bring the milk to a low boil and add the eggs and salt. Mix the milk mixture with the onions and stir in the cheese. Pour slowly into the pie crust and bake at 300° for 50 to 60 minutes.

Julie Pennington

ONION RICE

1 c. white rice (do not use
    instant)
1 can Campbell's French
    onion soup

1 can water
½ c. butter (1 stick)

Preheat oven to 350°. Combine all ingredients in an oven-safe 8 x 8 glass dish. Bake for 1 hour.

Heather Cato

PINEAPPLE AND CHEESE CASSEROLE

2 large cans pineapple
    chunks, drained (reserve
    juice)
2 Tbsp. flour
½ c. sugar

1 to 2 c. shredded cheese
1 sleeve Ritz crackers,
    crushed
1 stick butter

Mix pineapple, 2 tablespoons of reserved juice, flour, sugar and cheese in large bowl. Mix melted butter and crackers in a separate bowl. Pour pineapple mixture in 13 x 9-inch baking dish. Top with cracker mixture. Bake at 350° for 30 minutes.

Michelle Bowden

CLASSIC PARMESAN SCALLOPED POTATOES

¼ c. butter
2 lb. Yukon Gold potatoes,
  peeled and thinly sliced
3 c. whipping cream (I used 2
  c. and then 1 c. half and
  half)
2 garlic cloves, chopped

1 ½ tsp. salt
¼ tsp. freshly ground pepper
¼ c. fresh flat-leaf parsley,
  chopped (optional)
½ c. (2 oz.) grated Parmesan
  cheese

Melt butter in a large Dutch oven over medium-high heat. Stir in potatoes and next 5 ingredients and bring to a simmering boil. Reduce heat to medium-low and cook, stirring gently, 15 minutes or until potatoes are tender. Spoon mixture into a lightly greased 13 x 9-inch baking dish; sprinkle with cheese. Bake at 400° for 25 to 30 minutes or until bubbly and golden brown. Remove to a wire rack and let stand 10 minutes before serving. Makes 6 to 8 servings.

Anita Geoghagan
Honorary Member

HASH BROWN CASSEROLE

2 (10 ¾ oz.) cans condensed
  cream of potato soup
1 c. sour cream
½ tsp. garlic salt

1 (2 lb.) pkg. frozen hash
  brown potatoes
2 c. shredded Cheddar cheese
½ c. Parmesan cheese

In large bowl, combine soup, sour cream and garlic salt. Add potatoes and cheeses. Mix well. Pour into a greased 13 x 9 x 2-inch baking dish. Bake uncovered at 350° for 55 to 60 minutes or until potatoes are tender.

Delane Stevens

HEAVENLY HASH BROWN CASSEROLE

2 lb. frozen hash browns,
  thawed
1 c. melted butter, divided
1 tsp. salt
½ tsp. pepper

½ c. chopped onion
1 can cream of chicken soup
2 c. sour cream
2 c. grated sharp Cheddar

Mix all and put into 9 x 13 pan. Mix 2 cups cornflakes, crushed, with ¼ cup butter and put on top. Bake at 350° for 45 minutes to 1 hour.

Kelly Brannam

ASHED POTATOES

5 lb. bag cooked Russet
  potatoes
1 ½ sticks butter

½ c. sour cream
¼ c. heavy whipping cream
salt and pepper

Mix all ingredients together with a hand mixer. Add as much salt and pepper as you want.

Kelley Hyde

$\mathscr{P}$ARMESAN BAKED POTATOES

5 lb. potatoes
1 pkg. cream cheese, softened
2 eggs
¾ tsp. salt (or more to taste)

½ tsp. pepper (or more to
  taste)
1 c. grated Parmesan cheese
½ c. bread crumbs
3 Tbsp. melted butter

Grease either a 2-quart or a 9 x 13 baking dish. Peel and cube the potatoes; cook until tender and then drain. Mash the potatoes; add the cream cheese, eggs, salt and pepper and ¾ cup of the Parmesan cheese. Place mixture into a greased 2-quart or 9 x 13 baking dish. Combine the bread crumbs, melted butter and remaining cheese and sprinkle over potatoes. Cover and refrigerate overnight.

Remove from refrigerator 30 minutes prior to baking. Preheat oven to 350°. Bake uncovered for 50 to 60 minutes, until center is set, hot and top is browned.

Julie Pennington

$\mathscr{P}$ARTY POTATOES

10 to 12 medium potatoes
1 (8 oz.) pkg. cream cheese,
  softened

1 small carton sour cream
4 Tbsp. butter or more
salt and pepper to taste

Pare potatoes, boil until tender and drain. Beat softened cream cheese, sour cream and butter. Add hot potatoes gradually, beating constantly until light and fluffy. Season with salt and pepper. Pour into 9 x 13-inch casserole dish. Bake at 350° for 25 minutes. Garnish with paprika and pats of butter, if desired. May be made several days ahead; refrigerate or freeze.

Beth Major

RED POTATO BAKE

3 ½ to 4 lb. red skinned
  potatoes
1 c. sour cream
¾ c. mayonnaise
salt and pepper to taste

2 c. Cheddar cheese,
  shredded
1 pack real bacon pieces
parsley flakes

Quarter potatoes or cut into large chunks. Boil potatoes until barely soft. Drain excess water immediately. Mix sour cream, mayonnaise, salt and pepper in bowl. Spoon over potatoes and gently cover until potatoes are covered. Sprinkle with cheese. Top with bacon pieces. Sprinkle lightly with parsley flakes. Bake at 350° until cheese is completely melted (approximately 15 minutes).

Velveeta cheese chunks may be substituted for shredded cheese, but baking time will increase in order to melt cheese thoroughly.

Sherry Wallace

ROASTED HERB BABY POTATOES

½ lb. small red skin potatoes,
  cleaned/scrubbed
½ lb. small white skin
  potatoes, cleaned/scrubbed
1 Tbsp. herbs de Provence

3 cloves garlic, minced
¼ c. extra virgin olive oil
salt and freshly ground
  black pepper

Preheat oven to 400°. Combine all the red and white potatoes in a large bowl. In a separate bowl, mix the herbs, garlic and oil together until thoroughly blended. Pour the mixture of herbs, garlic and oil over the potatoes. Sprinkle salt and black pepper and then toss potatoes to coat. Transfer the potatoes to a large baking dish, making sure they are spaced evenly across the dish. Roast the potatoes in the oven until tender and golden, turning occasionally, for about 1 hour. Remove and serve.

April Turner

STUFFED POTATOES

6 large potatoes
½ lb. sausage
1 small diced onion

4 Tbsp. butter
1 tsp. pepper
1 tsp. salt

Bake the potatoes in a 400° oven until well done (about 1 hour). While potatoes are baking, brown sausage lightly; add onion and leave on low heat until ready to use. Split the potatoes in half. Remove the insides, add salt, pepper and butter and mash thoroughly. More seasoning may be added to suit taste. Drain excess fat from sausage. Add the sausage mixture. Mix thoroughly and return to potato shells. Return to 400° oven until slightly browned.

Amy Howell

TWICE BAKED POTATO CASSEROLE

5 lb. Russet potatoes	**2 ½ c. Cheddar cheese,**
10 slices bacon	**grated**
8 oz. cream cheese	**1 tsp. salt**
½ c. sour cream	**½ tsp. pepper**
¼ c. chives, minced	

Preheat oven to 350°. Peel potatoes and cut into 1-inch chunks. Place in a large saucepan and add enough cold water to cover by about 2-inches. Bring to a boil over medium-high heat and reduce to a simmer. Cook until tender and easily pierced with a paring knife, about 20 minutes. Transfer to a colander to drain; return to pan, cover and set aside.

Meanwhile, heat a large skillet over medium heat. Add bacon and cook until crisp and browned, turning once. Transfer to paper towel to drain; let cool and crumble into pieces.

Using a fork, mash the potatoes in pan until light and fluffy. Add the cream cheese, butter and sour cream. Stir until combined and smooth. Add the chives, 2 cups of Cheddar cheese, half of the bacon, salt and pepper. Stir until well combined.

Transfer to a buttered 3-quart baking dish. Top with remaining ½ cup Cheddar cheese. Bake until top is slightly golden and potatoes are heated through, about 30 minutes. Remove from oven and top with remaining bacon. Serve immediately.

Laura Stanley

CANNON'S SWEET POTATO SOUFFLÉ

4 to 5 large sweet potatoes	**½ c. sugar**
1 stick butter, softened	**1 tsp. vanilla**
1 can sweetened condensed	**cinnamon and nutmeg to**
milk	**taste**
4 eggs	

Topping:

1 c. chopped pecans	**⅓ stick butter (firm)**
1 c. brown sugar	

Bake sweet potatoes until soft all the way through. Peel and add the stick of butter. Mash the two together until the butter is melted. Beat the eggs and vanilla together; add the sweetened condensed milk and sugar. Blend into the sweet potato mixture. Add spice to taste. Pour into a 9 x 13 pan and bake at 350° for 30 minutes.

While cooking, use a pastry blender to cut butter and brown sugar together. Mix in pecans. After removing sweet potatoes from oven, reduce oven heat to 325°, sprinkle topping on top of sweet potatoes and bake for 20 minutes.

The sweet potatoes part can be made ahead of time and frozen. When ready to use, defrost and add topping. Cook at 325° for 30 minutes.

Jory Cannon
Honorary Member

SOUTHERN SWEET POTATO SOUFFLÉ

3 c. mashed sweet potatoes (fresh or canned)	2 eggs
	1/3 stick margarine
1 c. sugar	1/2 c. milk
1/2 tsp. salt	1 tsp. vanilla

Mix all ingredients together and pour into greased baking dish. Cover with topping.

Topping:

1 c. brown sugar	1 c. chopped pecans
1/3 c. flour	1/3 c. melted margarine

Mix thoroughly and sprinkle over soufflé. Bake at 350° for approximately 45 minutes.

Ashley Rusbridge

TRADITIONAL SWEET POTATO SOUFFLE

2 c. cooked sweet potatoes	dash of cinnamon
3/4 stick margarine	1 c. canned evaporated milk
2 eggs	1/2 c. sugar

Topping:

3/4 c. crushed corn flakes	1/2 c. brown sugar
1/2 c. chopped pecans	3/4 stick margarine

Mix sweet potatoes, margarine, eggs, cinnamon, evaporated milk and sugar. Pour in 9 x 13 glass baking dish.

Mix all topping ingredients and pour over sweet potato mixture. Bake 15 to 20 minutes at 400°.

Kelley Hyde

BROWN RICE CASSEROLE

1 can beef consommé soup	1/2 stick butter
1 can French onion soup	1 c. long grain rice

Spray 9 x 13 baking dish. Pour all ingredients into dish and mix. Bake at 350° for 45 minutes.

Kim Fowler

MUSHROOM RICE PILAF

1 c. uncooked white rice	5 large green onions (white
1 tsp. salt	part only), thinly sliced
½ lb. mushrooms, sliced	¼ c. butter or margarine
	2 c. canned chicken broth

Place rice and salt in 2-quart casserole dish and set aside. In large saucepan, sauté mushrooms and onions in butter until tender, stirring occasionally. Add chicken broth and bring to a boil. Pour over rice and cover dish. Bake at 350° for 25 to 30 minutes, until rice is tender and liquid is absorbed. Let stand for 5 minutes, fluff with fork and enjoy!

Wendy Landry

SEASONED BROWN RICE

1 can Campbell's beef	1 c. white rice
consommé soup	1 c. water
1 stick margarine	

Melt margarine in a 9 x 13 dish. Add soup, rice and water. Cover with foil. Cook at 350° for 45 minutes to 1 hour. Stir and serve.

Kaye Rogers
Honorary Member

SUMMER SQUASH CASSEROLE

1 ½ lb. yellow squash	1 (8 oz.) container sour
1 lb. zucchini	cream
1 small sweet onion, chopped	1 ½ c. Cheddar cheese,
¼ c. grated carrots	shredded
1 (10 ½ oz.) can cream of	1 (8 oz.) bag herb seasoned
chicken soup	stuffing
	½ c. butter, melted

Cut squash and zucchini into ¼-inch thick slices and place in large pot. Add chopped onion and cover with water. Bring to a boil and cook for 5 minutes. Drain well. Combine carrots, cream of chicken soup, sour cream and shredded cheese. Carefully fold in squash and onion mixture. Mix just until combined.

In a separate dish, melt butter and combine with the bag of stuffing mix. Spoon ½ of stuffing mixture in bottom of lightly buttered 9 x 13-inch baking dish. Carefully top with squash mixture. Top with remaining stuffing mixture. Bake at 350° for 45 minutes or until bubbly and light brown.

Jodi Sears

$\mathcal{N}$ANA'S VEGETABLE CASSEROLE

1 can whole kernel corn	1 c. finely chopped green
1 can French-style green	pepper
beans	1 c. finely chopped onion
1 can cream of chicken soup	1 c. finely chopped celery
½ c. sour cream	1 stick butter
1 c. shredded Cheddar cheese	1 to 1 ½ sleeves Ritz crackers

Heat oven to 400°. Combine all ingredients, except for Ritz crackers and butter, in a large bowl. Stir until well mixed. Place stick of butter in a 9 x 11 casserole dish and heat until completely melted. Place the casserole mixture into the baking dish and bake about 45 minutes, stirring once at about 30 minutes. Casserole should be very bubbly when ready to remove from the oven.

Crumble the Ritz crackers on top of the casserole. Place casserole back in the oven (on broil) for an additional 3 minutes to brown the Ritz cracker crust. Use caution to not overbrown the cracker crust. Casserole is best if allowed to sit for about 15 minutes before serving.

Lynn Struck

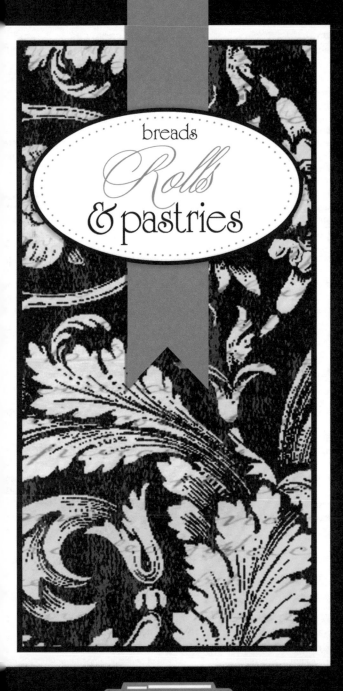

breads
Rolls
& pastries

Baking Tips

COMMON PROBLEMS (Common Failures)	CAUSES OF PROBLEMS (Causes of Failures)

Biscuits

Rough biscuits................................. — Insufficient mixing

Dry biscuits................................... — Baking in too slow an oven and handling too much

Uneven browning........................... — Cooking in dark surface pan, too high a temperature and rolling the dough too thin

Breads (yeast)

Porous bread.................................. — Over-rising or cooking at too low a temperature

Crust is dark and blisters just under the crust............................ — Under-rising

Bread does not rise........................ — Over-kneading or using old yeast

Bread is streaked........................... — Under-kneading and not kneading evenly

Bread bakes unevenly..................... — Using old, dark pans, too much dough in pan, crowding the oven shelf or cooking at too high a temperature

Cakes

Cracks and uneven surface............. — Too much flour, too hot an oven and sometimes from cold oven start

Dry cakes...................................... — Too much flour, too little shortening, too much baking powder or cooking at too low a temperature

Heavy cakes.................................. — Too much sugar or baking too short a period

Sticky crust................................... — Too much sugar

Coarse grained cake....................... — Too little mixing, too much shortening, too much baking powder, using shortening too soft, and baking at too low a temperature

Fallen cakes.................................. — Using insufficient flour, under baking, too much sugar, too much shortening or not enough baking powder

Uneven color................................. — Cooking at too high a temperature, crowding the shelf (allow at least 2 inches around pans) or using dark pans

Uneven browning........................... — Not mixing well

Cookies

Uneven browning........................... — Not using shiny cookie sheet or not allowing at least 2 inches on all sides of cookie sheets in oven

Soggy cookies............................... — Cooling cookies in pans instead of racks

Excessive spreading of cookies........ — Dropping cookies onto hot cookie sheets; not chilling dough; not baking at correct temperature

Muffins

Coarse texture............................... — Insufficient stirring and cooking at too low a temperature

Tunnels in muffins, peaks in center and soggy texture................... — Over-mixing

Pies

Pastry crumbles............................. — Over-mixing flour and shortening

Pastry tough.................................. — Using too much water and over-mixing the dough

Pies do not brown (fruit or custard).............................. — Bake at constant temperature (400-425 degrees) in Pyrex or enamel pie pan

BREADS, ROLLS & PASTRIES

$\mathscr{B}$ANANA BREAD

⅔ c. margarine, softened
1 ½ c. sugar
2 eggs
1 ½ c. all-purpose flour
2 tsp. baking powder

¼ tsp. salt
4 Tbsp. milk
1 c. bananas, mashed
½ c. pecans, chopped
1 tsp. vanilla extract

Cream together margarine and sugar. Add eggs. Sift flour, baking powder and salt together. Add flour mixture and milk to creamed ingredients. Stir in mashed bananas, pecans and vanilla. Pour into greased 9 x 5-inch loaf pan. Bake at 350° for 45 minutes. This recipe also freezes well for later use.

Wanda Roach
Honorary Member

$\mathscr{B}$EER BREAD

3 c. self-rising flour*
3 Tbsp. granulated sugar

1 (12 oz.) can beer

*Can substitute 3 cups all-purpose flour, 3 teaspoons baking soda and 1 ½ teaspoons salt for self-rising flour.

Preheat oven to 375°. Lightly spray loaf pan with cooking spray. Combine all ingredients, mixing well. Pour into pan and bake 1 hour.

Karen McClellan
Honorary Member

CHOCOLATE CHIP BANANA BREAD

1 c. sugar	2 c. sifted all-purpose flour
½ c. margarine	½ tsp. salt
2 large eggs	½ tsp. banana flavoring (if
1 tsp. vanilla	bananas are not overly
4 ripe bananas (need to be	ripe)
black and oozing)	1 c. chocolate chips
1 tsp. baking soda dissolved	
in ¼ c. water	

Cream sugar and margarine together. Add eggs one at a time. Mix in vanilla, bananas and baking soda and water mixture. Add flour and chocolate chips. Pour into 1 large or 2 regular sized greased loaf pan(s) and bake at 250° for 1 ½ hours or until middle is firm. (Best if served heated with butter.)

Lisa Woodruff

DAD'S OLD FASHIONED CORNBREAD

1 c. cornmeal (self-rising)	¼ tsp. black pepper
¾ c. flour (self-rising)	¼ c. canola oil
¼ tsp. salt	buttermilk

Preheat oven to 450°. Mix cornmeal, flour, salt, black pepper and canola oil together in a large bowl. Add buttermilk until the mixture reaches a thorough consistency (not runny). Pour into a round baking pan and bake until brown.

April Turner

PUMPKIN BREAD

3 c. sugar	½ tsp. baking powder
1 c. vegetable oil	½ tsp. salt
3 large eggs	1 tsp. ground cloves
1 (16 oz.) can pumpkin	1 tsp. ground cinnamon
3 c. flour	1 tsp. ground nutmeg
1 tsp. baking soda	

Preheat oven to 350°. Grease and flour two 9-inch loaf pans. Mix sugar, oil, eggs and pumpkin. In another bowl, mix flour, baking soda, baking powder, salt and spices. Add wet mixture into dry mixture in two batches. Bake 1 hour and 10 minutes.

Barbara Jacoby

$\mathcal{S}$POON BREAD

1 c. corn meal
½ tsp. salt
1 ½ c. boiling water
2 eggs, separated

1 Tbsp. melted butter
1 c. buttermilk
½ tsp. baking soda

Mix corn meal and salt. Add water and egg yolks; then add butter and buttermilk. Beat egg whites; add soda and fold into batter. Put in greased 2-quart baking dish. Bake 45 minutes at 325° and serve immediately.

JoAnne Knieriem

$\mathcal{S}$TRAWBERRY BREAD

1 c. butter, softened
2 c. sugar
5 large eggs
½ tsp. strawberry extract
½ tsp. vanilla extract

2 ¼ c. all-purpose flour
½ tsp. salt
½ c. sour cream
¾ c. chopped strawberries

Glaze:
1 c. confectioners sugar
2 Tbsp. milk

1 drop of red food coloring

Preheat oven to 350°. Butter and flour 2 loaf pans. Using a mixer, beat butter on medium until creamy. Gradually add sugar until fluffy; add eggs one at a time and beat well after each addition. Add extracts. Combine flour and salt in a small bowl and gradually add to butter mixture; beat just until combined. Stir in sour cream and strawberries. Divide batter between 2 pans. Bake for 55 to 60 minutes.

Cool in pan for 10 minutes; spoon glaze over warm bread. Let cool for 1 hour.

Emily Jobe

$\mathcal{S}$WEET POTATO BREAD

3 ⅓ c. self-rising flour
1 ½ tsp. salt
2 tsp. cinnamon
1 tsp. ginger
3 c. sugar

4 eggs
⅔ c. water
2 c. sweet potato pie filling
1 c. cooking oil

Combine all dry ingredients. Add remaining ingredients and mix well. Pour into two 9 x 5 greased and floured loaf pans. Bake at 350° for 1 hour.

Kelley Hyde

$\mathcal{A}$MOSS' WILLIAMSBURG BREAD

16 oz. cream cheese
2 pkg. crescent rolls
1 c. sugar

1 tsp. vanilla
1 egg yolk (save white)
cinnamon and sugar

Place 1 package of rolls in bottom of 9 x 13 pan, pressing together seams. In a bowl, cream together cheese, sugar, vanilla and yolk. Spread evenly over rolls. Arrange second layer of rolls over top of cheese mixture. Brush with egg white and sprinkle with cinnamon sugar. Bake 30 minutes at 350°. Serve warm with store bought caramel topping or cold as a coffee cake.

Cookbook Committee

$\mathcal{L}$OUISE ROACH'S CHICKEN DRESSING

4 c. cornbread, broken up
3 c. biscuits, broken up
5 pieces white bread, broken
   up
4 c. chicken broth
¾ c. water

2 tsp. sage
1 ½ c. celery, chopped
¾ c. onion, chopped
2 eggs, beaten
½ c. margarine, melted
salt and pepper to taste

Combine all ingredients; mix well. Pour into a 9 x 13-inch greased baking dish. Bake at 400° for 30 to 40 minutes or until done.

Judy Key
Honorary Member

$\mathscr{M}$OTHER'S DRESSING

¼ c. melted butter	5 slices white loaf bread,
¾ c. diced onions	broken into small pieces
6 c. crumbled Dressing	7 c. reduced sodium chicken
Cornbread	broth
3 c. crumbled Dressing	2 tsp. sage (or more to taste)
Biscuits	

Sauté onions in the melted butter. In a large bowl mix together the cornbread, biscuits, white bread and sautéed onions. Next add the chicken broth and stir well. Add the sage and again stir well. The mixture should be quite moist. More broth can be added if needed. Pour the mixture into a 9 x 13 lightly greased baking dish. Bake until golden brown at 350° for approximately 50 to 60 minutes.

Dressing Cornbread:

2 c. self-rising corn meal mix	¼ c. vegetable oil
1 ⅓ c. milk	2 eggs, lightly beaten

Mix all the ingredients and pour into a 9-inch greased baking pan. Bake at 450° for 20 minutes or until golden brown.

Dressing Biscuits:

1 c. self-rising flour	½ c. milk or buttermilk
2 Tbsp. shortening	

In a mixing bowl cut the shortening into the flour. Add the milk and stir well. Drop by spoonfuls into 6 well-greased sections of a muffin tin. Bake at 450° for about 11 minutes or until brown.

Molly Mercer

CHOCOLATE PALEO MUFFINS

1 c. almond flour
½ c. coconut flour
1 Tbsp. cocoa powder
½ tsp. baking soda
¼ tsp. salt
pinch of cinnamon
2 pouches of instant coffee
  granules

1 c. Enjoy Life chocolate
  chips, melted
¼ c. almond milk or coconut
  milk
½ c. honey or agave nectar
½ c. safflower oil or coconut
  oil
5 eggs, beaten

Sift all dry ingredients together in a large mixing bowl. Melt chocolate chips in a microwave-safe bowl 30 seconds at a time until completely melted. Add honey, almond milk, oil, eggs and melted chocolate chips to the dry ingredients. Mix with electric hand mixer until well blended.

Divide batter into lined muffin tins, filling the cups to almost full. Bake at 350° for 20 to 23 minutes or until top is cracking and a toothpick inserted in the center of each muffin comes out clean. Let cool for 5 minutes and remove from muffin pan and place on wire rack to cool completely. Store in airtight container once cooled up to one week.

Note: Gluten-free, dairy-free, soy-free recipe.

Lori Davis

COFFEE CAKE MUFFINS

1 ¾ c. flour
2 tsp. baking powder
1 tsp. baking soda
½ c. butter, softened

1 c. sugar
1 c. sour cream
1 tsp. vanilla
2 eggs

Crumb Topping:
1 c. brown sugar
1 c. flour
½ tsp. cinnamon

½ tsp. salt
½ c. butter

Preheat oven to 350°. Grease and flour a muffin pan (12 jumbo muffins or about 16 regular muffins).

To make crumb topping: Mix dry ingredients; then add butter and mix until large crumbs form.

To make muffins: Mix flour, baking powder and baking soda. In another bowl, beat butter, sugar, sour cream and vanilla until fluffy; beat in eggs one at a time and then add flour mixture about ½ a cup at a time until well blended.

Put half the batter into the pan and top with half the crumbs. Add the rest of the batter and top with the rest of the crumbs. Bake 30 minutes.

Barbara Jacoby

CORNMEAL ROLLS

⅓ c. cornmeal (stone-ground preferred)
½ c. sugar
2 tsp. salt
½ c. shortening
2 c. milk
1 pkg. active dry yeast
¼ c. warm water (110° to 115°)
2 beaten eggs
4 c. flour or more as needed
melted butter
cornmeal

Cook cornmeal, sugar, salt, shortening and milk in medium saucepan until thick (like cooked cereal). Cool to lukewarm. Add yeast which has been dissolved in lukewarm water, then eggs. Beat thoroughly. Add flour to form soft dough. Knead well on lightly floured surface. Place in bowl; cover; let rise. Punch down. Roll out to 1-inch thickness; cut with 2 ½-inch biscuit cutter. Brush with melted butter; dust with cornmeal. Place on greased cookie sheet; cover; let rise. Bake at 375° for 15 minutes. (Dough will keep in refrigerator for several days.) Yield: 18 rolls.

JoAnne Knieriem

EASY YEAST ROLLS

1 pack dry yeast
¼ c. warm water
½ c. shortening
⅓ c. sugar
1 egg
1 tsp. salt
1 c. warm water
4 to 5 c. flour

Mix yeast with ¼ cup warm water and set aside. Cream shortening and sugar. Add egg and salt and mix thoroughly. Stir in the 1 cup warm water and softened yeast. Gradually add 4 cups flour (more if needed, but should be sticky); mix well. Let rise, covered, in warm place until doubled in bulk. Punch down. Shape into rolls; place in greased pans and butter tops. Let rise again until doubled. Bake at 425° for 12 to 15 minutes.

Robyn McEntyre

GRAMMY'S BISCUITS

1 pkg. active dry yeast
1 c. warm water
2 Tbsp. sugar

1 stick butter, melted
1 tsp. baking powder
2 ½ to 3 ½ c. flour

Dissolve yeast in warm water; let sit for 10 minutes. Add sugar and 3 tablespoons melted butter, slowly stirring to incorporate. Add 2 cups flour and baking powder to liquid mixture. Mix well. If dough seems too "sticky," add additional ½ cup flour and mix again.

Turn dough out onto floured surface and knead about 3 minutes, adding small additional amounts of flour if dough is too sticky. Pat out the dough to ½-inch thickness. Cut with a biscuit cutter and dip in melted butter and place in an 8 x 11 dish. Once all biscuits have been cut and dipped in butter and placed in pan, pour any remaining melted butter over the top of the biscuits.

Let the dough sit and rise in a warm place for 1 hour. Bake at 400° for about 15 minutes or until golden brown.

Julie Pennington

SWEET POTATO BISCUITS

1 large sweet potato
2 c. self-rising flour
¼ c. sugar

3 Tbsp. shortening
2 Tbsp. butter, cut up
⅓ c. milk

Bake sweet potato at 350° for 1 hour or until tender; cool slightly. Peel and mash; cool. Combine flour and sugar in a medium bowl. Cut shortening and butter into flour mixture with a pastry blender until crumbly; add mashed sweet potato and milk, stirring just until dry ingredients are moistened. Turn dough out onto a lightly floured surface; knead 3 to 4 times. Roll dough to ½-inch thickness; cut with a 2-inch round cutter. Place on a lightly greased baking sheet. Bake at 400° for 15 minutes or until golden brown.

Anita Geoghagan
Honorary Member

CREAM CHEESE DANISH

2 pkg. refrigerated crescent
  rolls
2 pkg. cream cheese, softened
1 c. powdered sugar

1 tsp. vanilla
1 egg yolk
2 Tbsp. milk

Glaze:
¾ c. powdered sugar
1 Tbsp. milk

½ tsp. vanilla

Cream together cream cheese, powdered sugar, vanilla, egg yolk and milk. Line the bottom of a greased 9 x 13-inch oven-safe glass baking dish with 1 package of crescent rolls. Spread mixture over crescent rolls; then unroll second package of rolls onto top of mixture. Bake at 350° for 25 to 30 minutes.

Glaze: Mix everything together with a whisk. Drizzle glaze onto Danish and chill before cutting.

Lisa Woodruff

YOUR FAVORITE RECIPES

Recipe   Page Number

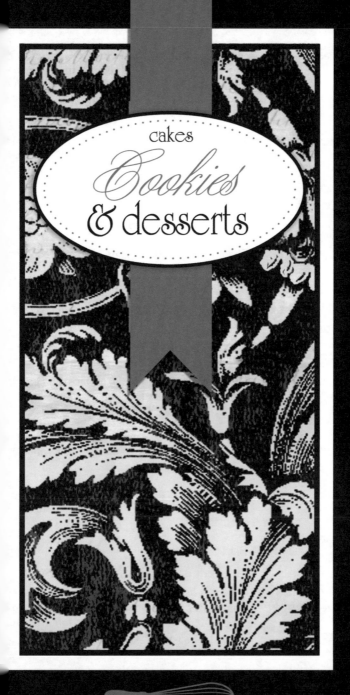

cakes
Cookies
& desserts

Candy Testing

Thermometer Test: Check candy thermometer in boiling water. If it doesn't register 212 degrees, add or subtract the same number of degrees in recipe. Always make sure candy thermometer is covered with liquid, not just foam. Clip it to the side of the pan after syrup boils.

Cold-Water Test: Remove candy from heat. Drop a little syrup into small bowl of very cold, but not ice cold, water. Use a fresh cupful of cold water for each test. Form into ball with fingers, if possible.

Candy	Degrees	Stage	Cold Water Test
	230-234	Thread	Syrup spins 2-inch thread when dropped from spoon
Fudge,	234-240	Soft Ball	Candy will roll into soft ball but Fondant quickly flattens when removed from water.
Divinity, Caramels	244-248	Firm Ball	Candy will roll into a firm ball (but not hard ball) which will not lose its shape upon removal from water.
Taffy	250-266	Hard Ball	Syrup forms hard ball, although it is pliable.
Butterscotch	270-290	Light Crack	Candy will form threads in water which will soften when removed from water.
Peanut Brittle	300-310	Hard Crack	Candy will form hard, brittle threads in water which will not soften when removed from water
Caramelized Sugar	310-321	Caramelized	Sugar first melts, then becomes a golden brown and forms a hard, brittle ball in cold water

CAKES, COOKIES & DESSERTS

HEIRLOOM CREAM CHEESE POUND CAKE

*1 pkg. cream cheese, softened
 (8 oz.)
3 sticks salted butter,
 softened (1 ½ c.)
3 c. sugar*

*3 c. plain all-purpose flour
6 eggs (allowed to be brought
 to room temperature)
1 tsp. vanilla extract*

Beat cream cheese, butter and sugar until fluffy. Add flour and egg alternately, beating well. Add vanilla; beat well. Pour into a lightly greased and floured 10-inch tube pan. Bake at 325° for 1 hour 30 minutes. Cool.

Cream Cheese Frosting:

*1 (8 oz.) pkg. cream cheese,
 softened
½ c. salted butter, softened*

*1 (16 oz.) box confectioners
 sugar
1 tsp. vanilla extract*

Beat cream cheese and butter until light and fluffy. Add confectioners sugar gradually, beating well. Add vanilla; beat well. Spread onto fully cooled Cream Cheese Pound Cake.

Molly Mercer

CREAM CHEESE POUND CAKE VARIATIONS

Aunt Carolyn's Coconut Cake:
1 tsp. coconut flavoring
½ c. coconut (or up to 1 c., if desired)

Prepare batter for Cream Cheese Pound Cake. Mix in, just until incorporated, coconut flavoring and coconut. Spoon batter into greased and floured tube pan and bake at 325° for 1 ½ hours.

Coconut Cream Cheese Pound Cake Frosting:

Prepare Cream Cheese Frosting. Spread frosting over completely cooled cake. Sprinkle top with ½ cup coconut. If desired, press additional (1 to 1 ½ cups) coconut to sides of cake.

Christmas Cake:
1 tsp. almond extract
½ tsp. coconut extract
12 chopped maraschino cherries, patted dry before chopping
⅓ c. pecans, toasted, cooled and coarsely chopped
¼ c. thawed coconut (Birds Eye brand frozen coconut is what I use)

Grease and flour 2 round 9-inch cake pans. Prepare batter for Cream Cheese Pound Cake. Once prepared, mix in listed ingredients, just until incorporated.
Preheat oven to 325°. Divide batter evenly into pans. Turn heat down to 310° and bake for 15 minutes; then bake at 320° for 10 minutes and finish baking at 310° for an additional 20 minutes, or until wooden pick comes out clean.

Christmas Cake Frosting:
1 tsp. almond extract
¼ c. white (clear) corn syrup (with vanilla flavoring is fine)
½ to ¾ c. toasted pecans, chopped (reserving a few halves for garnish)
⅓ (or more to taste) c. coconut

Prepare Cream Cheese Frosting. Mix in almond extract and corn syrup. Stir in toasted pecans and coconut. Spread frosting between layers of and over the top of completely cooled cakes. Garnish with pecan halves, a few cherries patted dry and a dusting of coconut, as desired.

Cinnamon Brown Sugar Cream Cheese Pound Cake:
1 tsp. ground cinnamon (or more to taste)
2 Tbsp. brown sugar
2 tsp. ground cinnamon
2 Tbsp. brown sugar
2 tsp. ground cinnamon

Prepare batter for Cream Cheese Pound Cake. Once prepared, mix in 1 teaspoon ground cinnamon just until incorporated. Spoon half of the batter into a greased and floured tube pan. Sprinkle a single layer of 2 tablespoons brown sugar and 2 teaspoons ground cinnamon. Spoon the other half of the batter on top of the first layer. Sprinkle on top 2 tablespoons brown sugar and 2 teaspoons cinnamon. Bake in a preheated oven at 325° for 1 ½ hours.

Petit Fours:

⅔ pkg. cream cheese, softened	*2 c. all-purpose flour*
2 sticks butter (1 c.), softened	*4 large eggs*
2 c. sugar	*⅔ tsp. vanilla extract*

Prepare ⅔ Cream Cheese Pound Cake in proportions listed. Pour prepared batter into a greased and floured 9 x 13 cake pan. Bake at 305° for 1 hour. Cool for 20 to 30 minutes; then flip cake out onto a long paper towel. Once completely cooled, wrap in paper towels and an outer tighter layer of aluminum foil. Place into freezer for 45 minutes prior to cutting into small cakes. (Chilling the cakes makes them less crumbly when cutting into cakes.)

To cut cakes: Lay kitchen towel onto working surface. Place wrapped cake on top and unwrap so that cake is bottom side up. (Leave foil and paper towels underneath cake while cutting for easier cleanup.) Using dental floss, measure and make impressions for a cutting guide if cutting into squares. Cut clean, broad strokes, best done with a long knife. Alternately, use a deep cookie cutter and punch out the cake shapes. For best results, use cutters with uncomplicated designs. (For example, for Easter, an egg shape works better than a bunny.)

Place punched out or cut out cakes onto a wire rack. Place a large clean baking sheet with raised edges beneath the rack. Mix your favorite glaze and pour over cakes. Allow cakes to drip for a few moments; then scrape (with a spatula) the excess glaze back into original pouring bowl. Repeat the process until all cakes are covered sufficiently with glaze on tops and on most sides of cakes.

To decorate: Pipe frosting or drizzle with a different color of glaze after allowing initial glaze to dry a few minutes. If using sprinkles to decorate, sprinkle as soon as possible for better "stick."

Molly Mercer

CHOCOLATE POUND CAKE

3 c. sugar
½ c. shortening
2 sticks margarine (Land O
 Lakes is the best)
3 c. sifted flour (Gold Medal
 all-purpose)
5 whole eggs

½ tsp. baking powder
½ c. cocoa
1 ¼ c. sweet milk (whole milk
 works best)
½ tsp. salt
2 tsp. vanilla

Cream together sugar, shortening and margarine. Add eggs, one at a time, mixing well after each. Sift together cocoa, baking powder, salt and sifted flour. Sift together a total of 3 times. Alternately add milk and dry ingredients to sugar mixture, beginning and ending with milk. Add vanilla. Bake in a greased and floured tube pan at 325° for 1 hour and 30 minutes.

Frosting:

1 stick margarine
4 Tbsp. cocoa
⅓ c. sweet milk

1 box powdered sugar
1 c. chopped pecans
1 tsp. vanilla

Stir together (using a whisk) in saucepan the margarine, cocoa and milk. Bring to a boil. Remove from heat. Blend in powdered sugar (sifted), nuts and vanilla. When smooth, spread on cake.

Lisa Woodruff

CHOCOLATE VELVET POUND CAKE

1 ½ c. semi-sweet chocolate
  morsels
½ c. butter, softened
1 (16 oz.) pkg. light brown
  sugar
3 large eggs
2 c. all-purpose flour

1 tsp. baking soda
½ tsp. salt
1 (8 oz.) container sour
  cream
1 c. hot water
2 tsp. vanilla extract

Melt semi-sweet chocolate morsels in a microwave-safe bowl at High for 30-second intervals until melted (about 1 ½ minutes total time). Stir until smooth. Beat butter and brown sugar at medium speed with an electric mixer, beating about 5 minutes or until well blended. Add eggs, 1 at a time, beating just until blended after each addition. Add melted chocolate, beating just until blended. Sift together flour, baking soda and salt. Gradually add to chocolate mixture alternately with sour cream, beginning and ending with flour mixture. Beat at low speed just until blended after each addition. Gradually add 1 cup hot water in a slow, steady stream, beating at low speed just until blended. Stir in vanilla.

Spoon batter evenly into a greased and floured 10-inch tube pan. Bake at 350° for 55 to 65 minutes or until a wooden pick inserted in center comes out clean. Cool in pan on a wire rack 10 minutes. Remove from pan and let cool completely on wire rack. Sift powdered sugar over top of cake.

Alison C. Higgins

COCONUT POUND CAKE

Cake:
1 ½ c. shortening
2 ½ c. sugar
5 eggs
1 c. milk
3 c. all-purpose flour

1 tsp. baking powder
¼ tsp. salt
2 tsp. coconut flavoring
1 (8 oz.) can flake coconut

Glaze (Optional):
1 c. sugar
½ c. water

1 tsp. coconut flavoring
¼ c. white corn syrup

Cake: Preheat oven to 325°. With a mixer on high speed, cream shortening and sugar for approximately 3 minutes. Sift flour, salt and baking powder together in a separate bowl. To shortening mixture, add eggs one at a time; then alternately add milk and flour mixture. Fold in coconut flavoring and coconut. Bake 1 hour and 15 minutes.

Glaze: Boil all ingredients on medium heat for 4 ½ minutes. Poke holes in hot cake while still in pan. Pour half of glaze over cake so it seeps into cake. Let cake stand in pan and cool for 10 minutes. Turn out of pan onto plate and pour remaining glaze over cake.

Melissa Whatley

ℰDNA IVY'S FIVE FLAVOR CAKE

1 c. butter or margarine
½ c. shortening
3 c. sugar
5 eggs, well beaten
3 c. all-purpose flour
½ tsp. baking powder
1 c. milk

1 tsp. coconut extract
1 tsp. rum extract
1 tsp. butter flavoring
1 tsp. lemon extract
1 tsp. vanilla extract
Glaze (optional)

Cream butter, shortening and sugar until light and fluffy. Add eggs. Combine flour and baking powder; add to creamed mixture alternately with milk. Stir in extracts. Spoon mixture into a greased and floured 10-inch Bundt or tube pan. Bake at 325° for 1 hour 15 minutes or until cake tests done.

Add Glaze, if desired. Pour ½ of Glaze while cake is in pan. Cool in pan about 10 minutes; remove. Pour remaining Glaze over cake.

Glaze:

1 c. sugar
½ c. water
1 tsp. coconut extract
1 tsp. rum extract

1 tsp. lemon extract
1 tsp. vanilla extract
1 tsp. almond extract

Combine all ingredients in a saucepan; bring to a boil, stirring until sugar is melted.

Judy Bishop
Honorary Member

ℱRESH PEACH POUND CAKE

½ lb. butter (at room
   temperature)
3 c. granulated sugar
6 eggs
3 c. all-purpose flour
¼ tsp. baking soda

½ c. sour cream
2 c. fresh peaches, pitted,
   peeled and chopped
1 tsp. almond flavoring
1 tsp. vanilla flavoring

Requires 3 bowls for mixing. Preheat oven to 350°. Make sure butter is at room temperature. Using large mixing bowl, beat butter and sugar until light and fluffy. Add eggs (1 at a time) to sugar/butter mixture and beat well between each addition. Mix flour and baking soda together in second bowl. In third bowl, combine peaches and sour cream. Add ⅓ of flour mixture to the sugar, butter and eggs. Mix well. Add ½ of peaches and sour cream mixture and mix well. Repeat these steps, ending with flour mixture. Add almond and vanilla flavorings. Pour into greased and floured tube pan and cook approximately 70 minutes at 350°.

Laura Stanley

LILLIE MAE BROWNLEE'S BROWN SUGAR POUND CAKE

2 sticks butter
½ c. Crisco
½ tsp. salt
1 box light brown sugar
5 whole eggs

1 c. milk
1 tsp. vanilla
3 c. cake flour
1 tsp. baking powder
1 c. black walnuts (optional)

Preheat oven to 350°. Cream together butter and Crisco. Add salt. Then gradually add brown sugar and 5 eggs separately. Then add the remaining ingredients. Pour into a Bundt cake pan and bake for 1 hour.

Mary Johnston
Honorary Member

LILLIE MAE BROWNLEE'S POUND CAKE

1 ¼ c. Crisco
2 ½ c. granulated sugar
3 c. sifted flour
5 eggs

1 c. milk
1 tsp. baking powder
1 tsp. vanilla extract
1 tsp. almond extract

Preheat oven to 325°. Mix all ingredients together and pour into a greased and floured Bundt cake pan. Bake for 1 hour and 20 minutes.

Mary Johnston
Honorary Member

NANA'S POUND CAKE

3 c. sugar
2 sticks butter (at room
  temperature)
½ c. Crisco

6 eggs (at room temperature)
3 c. all-purpose flour
1 c. evaporated milk
1 tsp. vanilla

Mix sugar, butter and Crisco together. Add 1 egg at a time. Add flour and milk, alternating each. Add vanilla. Mix all ingredients well. Spray pan with Pam. Bake at 300° for 90 minutes or until cake tester comes out clean.

Amy Graham

PINEAPPLE POUND CAKE

3 c. sugar
¼ tsp. salt
2 c. Crisco
10 eggs

3 c. plain flour
1 small can crushed
  pineapple, drained (reserve
  juice)

Glaze:
½ c. sugar
1 Tbsp. butter

reserved pineapple juice

Cream sugar and Crisco; add flour, 1 cup at a time, with 4 eggs. Add second cup of flour with 3 eggs; add the last cup of flour with the remaining 3 eggs. Add salt. Stir in pineapple with spatula and pour into a greased and floured tube pan. Bake at 300° for 1 ½ hours.

Glaze: Cook Glaze ingredients in a saucepan until thick when dropped from spoon. Spread over hot unmolded cake with a pastry brush.

Amy Howell

SOUR CREAM POUND CAKE

2 ¼ c. White Lily all-purpose
  flour
½ tsp. salt
¼ tsp. soda
2 sticks unsalted butter
  (room temperature)

3 c. sugar
6 extra large eggs
1 c. sour cream
½ tsp. vanilla extract
½ tsp. lemon extract
½ tsp. almond extract

Glaze:
⅓ c. lemon juice
2 c. confectioners sugar

2 Tbsp. butter, melted
1 Tbsp. water

Preheat oven to 325°. Grease and flour a 10-inch tube pan. Combine flour, salt and soda and set aside. Cream butter and sugar on medium speed 2 minutes, until fluffy and light. Add eggs one at a time. Beat 2 minutes. Alternate with dry ingredients and sour cream, beginning and ending with sour cream. Bake 1 hour 15 minutes at 325°. Cool on cake rack.

To make the Glaze: In a medium bowl, combine lemon juice and confectioners sugar. Beat in the melted butter and 1 tablespoon water. Poke holes in the top of the cake and pour glaze over.

Lisa Woodruff

SOUTHERN PRALINE PECAN CAKE

1 box Betty Crocker pecan cake mix	4 eggs, beaten
	¾ c. oil
1 carton Betty Crocker coconut pecan frosting	1 c. water
	1 c. chopped pecans, divided

Mix all ingredients, except pecans. Stir in ½ pecans. Spray Bundt pan with nonstick spray. Sprinkle remaining ½ pecans into prepared Bundt pan. Add batter and bake at 350° for 50 minutes.

Beth Major

THIRTY POUND CAKE

1 c. shortening	½ tsp. baking powder
2 c. sugar	¾ tsp. salt
4 eggs	1 tsp. vanilla
3 c. plain flour	1 tsp. lemon extract
½ tsp. soda	1 c. buttermilk

Cream shortening with sugar. Add eggs, one at a time. Sift dry ingredients together and add alternately with buttermilk to first mixture. Add vanilla and lemon extract. Bake in greased and floured tube pan or two loaf pans at 350° for 1 hour and 20 minutes (tube pan) or 45 minutes (loaf pans).

Mary Johnston
Honorary Member

$\mathcal{W}$HITE WINE CAKE

Cake:

1 (18 ¾ oz.) box yellow cake
mix
1 (3.4 oz.) box instant vanilla
pudding mix
¼ c. light brown sugar
¼ c. granulated sugar

2 tsp. cinnamon
¾ c. vegetable oil
¼ c. white wine
4 eggs
¾ c. water

Glaze:

½ c. margarine (not butter)
1 c. granulated sugar

¼ c. white wine

Preheat oven to 325°. Mix cake mix, pudding mix, brown sugar, granulated sugar, cinnamon, oil, wine, eggs and water together with a mixer. Pour into a greased and floured Bundt pan. Bake for 60 to 75 minutes.

To make glaze, melt the margarine slightly in a saucepan. Remove from heat and add sugar. Mix together well. Bring to a boil for 3 to 4 minutes. Remove from heat and slowly add wine.

Poke holes in the cake with a fork while it is still in the pan. Spoon ¾ of the glaze over the cake. Let stand 10 minutes. Invert and remove from the pan. Spoon remaining glaze over the top.

If desired, ¼ cup chopped pecans may be added to the Bundt pan before adding the cake mixture.

Beth Brandon
Honorary Member

AUNT HILDA'S COCONUT LAYER CAKE

1 c. Crisco
2 c. sugar
4 eggs
½ tsp. salt

1 tsp. baking soda
2 ½ c. plain flour
1 c. buttermilk
1 tsp. vanilla

Cream Crisco and sugar until fluffy. Add eggs one at a time. Sift together salt, baking soda and flour. Add alternately to mixture with milk and beat until smooth. Add vanilla. Pour into three 9-inch greased and floured pans. Bake at 350° for 30 to 40 minutes. Cool and then frost.

Icing:

1 ½ c. sugar
⅓ c. water
¼ tsp. cream of tartar
¼ tsp. salt
2 egg whites

1 tsp. vanilla
8 oz. can coconut (fresh is best, but can type works fine too)

Mix sugar, water, cream of tartar, salt and egg whites in top of double boiler. Beat over boiling water for 7 to 10 minutes, until glossy white and firm. Take off water, add vanilla and beat another minute. Spread onto cake and sprinkle desired amount of coconut on top and sides.

Lisa Woodruff

BEST EVER WHITE CAKE

1 cake mix (white with pudding)
1 ¼ c. buttermilk
¼ c. melted butter

2 eggs
1 Tbsp. lemon rind
½ tsp. vanilla extract
½ tsp. almond extract

Grease and flour two 9-inch cake pans. Beat first 4 ingredients at low speed. Beat at medium speed 3 to 4 minutes. Stir in rind and flavorings. Bake at 350° for 35 to 40 minutes or until toothpick comes out clean.

Frosting:

8 oz. pkg. cream cheese
1 c. powdered sugar

½ c. regular sugar
12 oz. Cool Whip

Beat cream cheese, powdered sugar and sugar until creamy. Fold into Cool Whip. Spread onto cake.
Note: If desired, add 8 milk chocolate candy bars with almonds chopped up into the frosting.

Wanda Roach
Honorary Member

$\mathcal{B}$ETTY'S COCONUT CAKE

3 c. sifted cake flour (sift;   2 c. sugar
  then measure)   4 eggs (unbeaten)
3 tsp. baking powder   1 tsp. vanilla flavoring
½ tsp. salt   ½ tsp. almond flavoring
1 c. butter   1 c. milk

Sift together presifted and measured flour, baking powder and salt. Cream butter until very soft. Add sugar, 2 tablespoons at a time, creaming after each addition until light and fluffy (will require total of approximately 10 minutes on mixer). Add eggs, one at a time, beating well after each. Add flavorings. Add flour mixture alternately with milk, beating until smooth. Bake at 350° in three 9-inch layer pans, greased, floured and lined on bottoms with wax paper, 35 minutes or until done and lightly browned.

Frosting:

3 egg whites   1 ½ tsp. vanilla extract
2 ¼ c. sugar   1 can crushed pineapple
⅛ tsp. salt   1 bag sweetened shredded
½ c. water   coconut
1 Tbsp. light corn syrup

Place egg whites, sugar, salt, water and corn syrup in the top of a double boiler. Place pan over boiling water. Do not touch the bottom of the pan with the mixer; beat constantly on high speed with electric mixer for 7 minutes; then beat in vanilla for 1 more minute.

Mix 2 cups of the frosting with 1 can crushed pineapple (well drained). This is your filling to spread on top of the bottom and middle layers.

Spread top layer and sides of cake generously with frosting and then cover completely with sweetened shredded coconut.

Julie Little

CARROT CAKE

2 c. granulated sugar	2 tsp. baking soda
1 ⅓ c. vegetable oil	1 ½ tsp. kosher salt
3 extra large eggs (room	1 c. raisins
temperature)	1 c. chopped walnuts
1 tsp. pure vanilla extract	1 lb. carrots, grated
2 ½ c. plus 1 Tbsp.	½ c. drained pineapple
all-purpose flour, divided	tidbits
2 tsp. ground cinnamon	

Preheat oven to 350°. Butter 2 (8-inch) round cake pans. Line with parchment paper; then butter and flour the pans. Beat the sugar, oil and eggs together in the bowl of an electric mixer until light yellow. Add the vanilla. In another bowl, sift together 2 ½ cups flour, the cinnamon, baking soda and salt. Add the dry ingredients to the wet ingredients. Toss the raisins and walnuts with 1 tablespoon flour. Fold in the carrots and pineapple. Add to the batter and mix well.

Divide the batter equally between the 2 pans. Bake for 55 to 60 minutes, or until a toothpick comes out clean. Allow the cakes to cool completely in the pans set over a wire rack.

Frosting:

¾ lb. cream cheese (room	1 tsp. vanilla
temperature)	1 lb. confectioners sugar,
½ lb. unsalted butter (room	sifted
temperature)	

Mix the cream cheese, butter and vanilla in the bowl of an electric mixer until just combined. Add the sugar and mix until smooth. Frost and enjoy the best carrot cake ever!

Dianne Murphy
Honorary Member

$\mathcal{L}$ILLIE MAE BROWNLEE'S GERMAN SWEET CHOCOLATE CAKE

*1 pkg. (4 oz.) Baker's German
   sweet chocolate
½ c. boiling water
1 c. butter or margarine
2 c. sugar
4 egg yolks
1 tsp. vanilla*

*2 ½ c. sifted Swans Down
   cake flour
1 tsp. baking soda
½ tsp. salt
1 c. buttermilk
4 egg whites, stiffly beaten*

Melt chocolate in boiling water. Cool. Cream butter and sugar until fluffy. Add yolks, one at a time; beat well after each. Blend in vanilla and chocolate. Sift flour with soda and salt; add alternately with buttermilk chocolate mixture, beating after each addition until smooth. Fold in beaten whites. Pour into three 8-inch cake pans, lined on bottom with parchment paper. Bake at 350° for 30 to 40 minutes. Cool. Frost as desired.

*Mary Johnston
Honorary Member*

$\mathcal{C}$OCONUT PECAN FROSTING

*1 can (12 oz.) evaporated
   milk
1 c. sugar
¾ c. (1 ½ sticks) butter or
   margarine*

*4 egg yolks, slightly beaten
2 tsp. vanilla
1 pkg. (7 oz.) coconut
1 ½ c. chopped pecans*

Mix milk, sugar, margarine, egg yolks and vanilla in large saucepan. Cook and stir on medium heat about 12 minutes or until thickened and golden brown. Remove from heat. Stir in coconut and pecans. Cool to room temperature and of spreading consistency. Makes about 4 ½ cups.

Kim McCurry-Barger

MARY WINSLOW'S HUMMINGBIRD CAKE

3 c. all-purpose flour	1 ½ tsp. vanilla extract
2 c. sugar	1 (8 oz.) can crushed
1 tsp. baking soda	pineapple (undrained)
1 tsp. salt	1 ½ c. pecans, chopped,
1 tsp. cinnamon	divided
3 eggs, beaten	2 c. bananas, chopped
1 c. vegetable oil	Cream Cheese Frosting

Combine flour, sugar, baking soda, salt and cinnamon. Add eggs and oil, stirring until dry ingredients are moistened. Do not beat. Stir in vanilla, pineapple, 1 cup pecans and bananas. Pour into greased and floured 9-inch cake pans. Bake at 350° for 25 to 30 minutes. Cool.

Cream Cheese Frosting:

¼ c. butter, softened	1 (16 oz.) box confectioners
1 (8 oz.) pkg. cream cheese,	sugar
softened	2 tsp. vanilla extract

Combine all ingredients. Beat until smooth. Spread Cream Cheese Frosting between layers and on sides and top. Top with ½ cup pecans.

Lisa Woodruff

ORANGE PINEAPPLE CAKE

Cake:

yellow cake mix (any brand)
½ c. oil
4 large eggs

1 (15 oz.) can mandarin
  oranges in light syrup,
  drained (reserve syrup)

Frosting:

1 (20 oz.) can crushed
  pineapple in light syrup
  (Dole)
1 large tub (not extra large)
  Cool Whip

1 Jell-O cheesecake mix
8 oz. sour cream
2 Tbsp. sugar

Mix dry cake mix, oranges (drain half the syrup off), oil and eggs with mixer. Grease 3 round cake pans (3 layer cake--this cake is best if it is 3 layers) and pour cake mixture into pans. Bake cake at temperature and amount of time per the directions on the cake mix box (typically 350° oven for 30 minutes). Test cake for doneness before removing from oven. Remove the cake from oven and let it cool for 45 minutes before frosting.

Cake Frosting: Mix the dry Jell-O cheesecake mix, sour cream, sugar, Cool Whip and pineapple. Mix with mixer until well blended. Frost cooled cake layers (frost between layers and top of cake and sides). Refrigerate cake for minimum of 6 hours before serving. Serves 10 to 12 people. Cake must be refrigerated after serving.

Jana Anderman

$\mathcal{M}$IMI'S PINK STRAWBERRY CAKE

Cake:
1 box white cake mix (not yellow or Butter Recipe)
1 small box strawberry Jell-O
2/3 c. frozen strawberries sliced in syrup, thawed and mashed

½ c. water
1 c. vegetable oil
4 eggs
1 Tbsp. vanilla flavoring

Icing:
1 box 10x confectioners sugar
1 stick margarine or butter, softened

1/3 c. strawberries (usually what is left from frozen pkg.)
1 tsp. vanilla flavoring

Cake: Mix cake mix and dry Jell-O mix. Add wet ingredients and follow mixing directions on cake mix box. Bake at 350° for 45 minutes for 9 x 13 pan or about 35 minutes for 4 round cake pans or less for cupcakes. Turn cake out of pan and let cool completely.

Icing: Mix all ingredients for icing and spread over cake or cupcakes.

Melissa Whatley

$\mathcal{T}$HE BEST CHOCOLATE CAKE

1 (18 ¼ oz.) box devil's food cake mix
1 (3.9 oz.) pkg. instant chocolate pudding mix
1 c. sour cream (regular or light)
1 c. milk

½ c. vegetable oil
½ c. water
4 eggs
3 c. (about 18 oz.) chocolate chips, divided
6 Tbsp. (¾ stick) butter

Preheat oven to 350°. Grease and flour a 10-inch Bundt pan. In a large bowl, combine cake mix, pudding mix, sour cream, milk, oil, water and eggs. Beat until blended and then mix in 2 cups chocolate chips. Pour batter into prepared pan. Bake for 40 to 50 minutes, or until toothpick inserted in center of cake comes out clean. Cool 15 minutes in the pan; then turn out onto a wire rack. Cool completely.

To make glaze: Melt butter in a saucepan over medium heat or in the microwave. Add 1 cup chocolate chips and stir until smooth. Drizzle over the cake.

Wanda Roach
Honorary Member

$\mathcal{A}$PPLE CARAMEL CAKE

1 pkg. yellow cake mix	1 c. packed brown sugar
1 ¼ c. oats (quick cook)	½ c. pecans, chopped
¾ c. butter, chilled	(optional)
1 egg	½ c. caramel ice cream
5 to 6 Granny Smith apples	topping

Preheat oven to 375°. Grease a 9 x 13 pan. Combine cake mix and oats. Cut in butter with a pastry blender until mixture resembles coarse crumbs. Reserve 1 ½ cups for topping. Add the egg to the remaining crumb mixture and mix well. Place in the bottom of the cake pan and press down.

Peel and slice apples, cutting into thin slices. Toss the apples with the brown sugar and pecans if desired. Layer apples over crust and sprinkle with the reserved crumb mixture. Bake for 30 minutes or until apples are tender. Drizzle the caramel ice cream topping over the top. Great with ice cream.

Julie Pennington

$\mathcal{B}$LUEBERRY APPLE DUMP CAKE

1 can blueberry pie filling	1 cake mix (yellow)
1 can apple pie filling	1 to 2 sticks butter
1 can crushed pineapple	
(just juice)	

Spread apple filling in pan, then blueberry on top of that. Pour all the juice out of the can of pineapple over fruit mixture. Pour cake mix evenly over fruit and juice mixture. Melt butter and pour over the dish. Bake at 350° for about 45 minutes.

Kim Fowler

CHOCOLATE CAKE

Cake:
1 stick margarine	2 c. sifted flour
1 c. water	1 tsp. baking soda
6 Tbsp. cocoa	½ c. buttermilk
½ c. Crisco	2 eggs
2 c. sugar	1 tsp. vanilla

Combine first 4 ingredients in pan and boil 1 minute. In a large mixing bowl, combine sugar, sifted flour and baking soda. Pour hot liquid over this; mix well. Add buttermilk, eggs and vanilla. Pour into greased and floured 9 x 13-inch pan and bake at 400° for 30 minutes.

Frosting:
1 stick oleo margarine	1 tsp. vanilla
6 Tbsp. cocoa	1 box powdered sugar
6 Tbsp. evaporated milk	chopped nuts

Bring oleo, cocoa and evaporated milk to boil. Pour over and mix with the powdered sugar and vanilla. Beat until thick. Spread on cake in pan. Sprinkle with chopped nuts.

Mary Johnston
Honorary Member

COCA-COLA CAKE

Cake:

2 c. granulated sugar
2 c. all-purpose flour
1 ½ c. small marshmallows
½ c. butter or margarine
½ c. vegetable oil
3 Tbsp. unsweetened cocoa
   powder

1 c. Coca-Cola
1 tsp. baking soda
½ c. buttermilk
2 large eggs
1 tsp. vanilla extract

Frosting:

½ c. butter
3 Tbsp. unsweetened cocoa
   powder
6 Tbsp. Coca-Cola

1 (16 oz.) box confectioners
  sugar
1 tsp. vanilla extract
1 c. chopped pecans

To prepare the cake: Preheat oven to 350°. In a bowl, sift sugar and flour. Add marshmallows. In saucepan, mix butter, oil, cocoa and Coca-Cola. Bring to a boil and pour over dry ingredients; blend well. Dissolve baking soda in buttermilk just before adding to batter, along with eggs and vanilla extract, mixing well. Pour into a well-greased 9 x 13-inch pan and bake 35 to 45 minutes. Remove from oven and frost immediately.

To prepare frosting: Combine butter, cocoa and Coca-Cola in a saucepan. Bring to a boil and pour over confectioners sugar, blending well. Add vanilla extract and pecans. Spread over hot cake. When cool, cut into squares and serve.

Laura Stanley

GG'S FRESH APPLE CAKE

2 c. sugar
1 ¼ c. oil
3 eggs
3 c. flour
2 tsp. cinnamon (optional)
1 tsp. salt

2 tsp. baking soda
2 tsp. vanilla
1 tsp. baking powder
1 c. chopped pecans
4 c. apples, finely diced

Grease 9 x 13 cake pan and preheat oven to 325°. Combine the sugar and oil and beat for 1 minute on medium-high. Add in eggs, one at a time; beat until light and fluffy. Mix in the remaining ingredients except the pecans and apples. The batter will be very thick. Fold in the apples and pecans. Pour into the greased baking dish and bake at 325° for 1 hour and 12 minutes to 1 hour and 30 minutes.

Julie Pennington

*M*IMI'S COFFEE CAKE

1 stick margarine	1 tsp. baking soda
1 c. sugar	1 tsp. baking powder
2 eggs	½ tsp. salt
1 tsp. vanilla	1 c. sour cream
2 c. flour	

Cream margarine and sugar. Add eggs, one at a time; then add vanilla. Mix 2 cups flour with baking soda, baking powder and salt. Add flour mixture to creamed mixture alternately with sour cream. Begin and end with the flour.

Topping:

½ c. brown sugar	1 tsp. cinnamon
¼ c. white sugar	1 c. chopped pecans

Mix together topping ingredients.

Spread ½ batter into a baking dish; top with ½ topping; then repeat (11 x 7 or 9 x 10 pan). Bake at 350° for 45 minutes.

Lisa Woodruff

*O*OEY GOOEY BUTTER CAKE

1 box yellow cake mix	8 oz. cream cheese
1 stick butter, melted	1 lb. powdered sugar
4 eggs	

Melt butter in cake pan in a 350° oven; then pour into a bowl. Mix cake mix and 2 eggs; then pour into cake pan. Soften cream cheese and mix with 2 eggs and powdered sugar. Spread cream cheese mixture on top of the cake mix. Bake at 350° for 50 minutes or until edges are brown and the middle has sunk. Do not overcook; overcooking will cause it to become dry, and it should be gooey.

Lori Davis

$\mathcal{T}$URTLE CAKE

1 German chocolate cake mix
  plus ingredients listed on
  box
1 (14 oz.) pkg. caramels
1 (5 oz.) can evaporated milk

¾ c. butter
1 c. chopped pecans
1 c. semi-sweet chocolate
  chips

Preheat oven to 350°. Grease a 9 x 13 cake pan. Mix the cake mix according to the package directions. Pour a little less than ½ of the batter into the prepared pan and bake for 15 minutes. Remove from the oven.

In a large saucepan, melt the caramels, butter and milk over low heat. Pour this mixture over the half baked cake. Sprinkle with pecans and chocolate chips. Pour remaining cake batter on top. Bake for an additional 25 to 30 minutes or until cake is set.

Julie Pennington

$\mathcal{A}$MARETTO CHEESECAKE

Crust:

1 ½ c. graham cracker
  crumbs
2 Tbsp. sugar

1 tsp. cinnamon
¼ c. + 2 Tbsp. margarine,
  melted

Combine crumbs, sugar, cinnamon and butter; mix well. Press onto bottom and halfway up sides of 9-inch spring-form pan. Chill.

Filling:

3 (8 oz.) pkg. cream cheese,
  softened
1 c. sugar
4 eggs
⅓ c. + 1 Tbsp. Amaretto,
  divided

1 (8 oz.) carton sour cream
1 Tbsp. + 1 tsp. sugar
¼ c. almonds, sliced
  (optional)
1 (1.2 oz.) chocolate candy
  bar, grated (optional)

Beat cream cheese until fluffy. Gradually add 1 cup sugar, mixing well. Add eggs, one at a time, beating well after each. Stir in ⅓ cup Amaretto; pour into prepared pan. Bake at 375° for 45 to 50 minutes or until set.

Combine sour cream, 1 tablespoon plus 1 teaspoon sugar and 1 tablespoon Amaretto; stir well. Spoon over cheese cake. Bake at 500° for 5 minutes. Cool to room temperature. Refrigerate for 24 to 48 hours. (Best when thoroughly chilled.) Garnish with almonds and grated chocolate, if desired.

Linda Hasty
Honorary Member

CHEESECAKE

1 pkg. graham cracker
  crumbs
1 ½ sticks margarine, melted
1 ½ c. sugar

1 (8 oz.) pkg. cream cheese,
  softened
5 eggs
1 ½ tsp. vanilla

Topping:
1 ½ pt. sour cream
½ c. sugar

1 ½ tsp. vanilla

Mix graham cracker crumbs and melted margarine and pour into a 9 x 13-inch pan. Combine sugar, cream cheese, eggs and vanilla. Mix well and pour over crust. Bake for 50 minutes at 325°.

When done add topping. Mix sour cream, sugar and vanilla. Mix well and pour over cheesecake and bake 10 more minutes. If desired, when cool add sliced strawberries, blueberries and kiwifruit.

Kelley Hyde

CHOCOLATE CHIP CHEESECAKE

Crust:
2 ½ c. graham cracker
  crumbs
¼ c. sugar

½ tsp. cinnamon
½ c. butter, melted

Combine all ingredients. Press onto bottom and halfway up sides of a 9 ½-inch spring-form pan. Chill.

Filling:
8 oz. semi-sweet chocolate
  chips
5 (8 oz.) pkg. cream cheese,
  softened
1 ¾ c. sugar

¼ c. all-purpose flour
1 tsp. vanilla extract
6 eggs
¼ c. half and half

Chop chocolate chips in a food processor; set aside. Blend together cream cheese, sugar, flour and vanilla until smooth in a processor or with a mixer. Add eggs, one at a time, beating after each. Stir in chocolate and half and half. Pour into shell. Bake at 275° for 2 hours 30 minutes. Cool. Chill overnight covered.

Linda Hasty
Honorary Member

ℬLUEBERRY PIE

8 oz. sour cream	1 egg, beaten
2 Tbsp. plain flour	2 ½ c. fresh or frozen
¾ c. sugar	blueberries
¼ tsp. salt	2 tsp. vanilla

Mix first 4 ingredients well. Mix next 3 ingredients together; then mix well with sour cream mixture. Pour into unbaked deep-dish frozen pie crust and bake at 400° for 25 minutes.

3 Tbsp. plain flour	3 Tbsp. chopped pecans
2 Tbsp. softened butter	3 Tbsp. sugar

Mix ingredients well and crumble over pie. Return to oven for 10 minutes or until slightly browned.

Jodi Sears

𝒞HOCOLATE PECAN PIE

1 refrigerated pie crust	½ c. firmly packed brown
1 (2 oz.) bar bittersweet	sugar
chocolate, chopped	4 large eggs
¼ c. heavy whipping cream	2 Tbsp. butter, melted
¾ c. light corn syrup	¼ tsp. salt
½ c. granulated sugar	2 c. chopped pecans

Preheat oven to 350°. On a lightly floured surface, roll out dough into a 12-inch circle. Fit into a 9-inch deep-dish pie plate, crimping edges if desired. Line crust with parchment paper; cover bottom of crust with pie weights. Bake for 8 minutes. Remove parchment and pie weights.

In a small saucepan, combine chocolate and cream. Cook over medium-low heat, stirring frequently, until chocolate mixture is smooth. Pour chocolate mixture into prepared pie crust. Chill for 30 minutes.

In a medium bowl, combine corn syrup and next 5 ingredients, whisking until smooth. Stir in pecans. Spoon batter over chocolate mixture. Bake for 1 hour or until center is set, covering pie with aluminum foil halfway through baking time to prevent excess browning if necessary. Cool completely before serving.

Wanda Roach
Honorary Member

CHOCOLATE TOWN PIE

½ c. butter or margarine,
   softened (Land O Lakes
   margarine is preferred)
2 eggs, beaten
2 tsp. vanilla extract
1 c. sugar
½ c. all-purpose flour
1 c. semi-sweet mini
   chocolate chips
1 c. chopped pecans
1 (9-inch) frozen unbaked pie
   shell

Preheat oven to 350°. In a small bowl, cream butter, eggs and vanilla. Combine sugar and flour and add to creamed mixture. Stir in chips and nuts and pour into an unbaked 9-inch pie shell. Bake for 45 to 50 minutes or until brown. Serve warm with topping or ice cream.

Lisa Woodruff

CRANBERRY NUT PIE

1 c. flour
½ c. white sugar
½ c. brown sugar
½ tsp. salt
2 c. cranberries (fresh)
½ c. chopped walnuts or
   pecans
½ c. butter, melted
2 eggs, beaten
1 tsp. vanilla

Grease 9-inch pie pan. Preheat oven to 350°. Mix flour, sugars and salt together. Toss the cranberries and nuts in the flour mixture until coated. Mix melted butter, eggs and vanilla together. Mix the egg mixture into the flour mixture until combined. Pour into pie pan and bake for 40 minutes, until a toothpick comes out clean.

Jory Cannon
Honorary Member

DIRT PIE

8 oz. cream cheese, softened
½ c. butter, softened
1 large (12 oz.) tub Cool
   Whip
1 c. powdered sugar
3 c. milk
2 medium boxes vanilla
   instant pudding
1 large bag Oreo cookies,
   crushed

Mix cream cheese and butter. Add Cool Whip and powdered sugar. Set aside. In separate bowl, mix milk and vanilla pudding. Combine 2 mixtures and mix well. Alternate crushed Oreos and pudding/cream cheese mixture in a glass bowl, ending with Oreos on top. Refrigerate for about 1 hour before serving.

Laura Stanley

$\mathcal{G}$RANNY B'S CHOCOLATE PIE

1/3 c. flour (self-rising)	2 c. milk
2/3 c. sugar	1 tsp. vanilla
2 heaping Tbsp. cocoa	2 Tbsp. butter
pinch of salt	1 pie crust
2 eggs	

Preheat oven to 350°. Brown pie crust in 350° oven just until slightly brown; watch closely. Mix flour, sugar, chocolate and salt. Separate egg yolks from whites. Add ½ cup of milk to yolks; then add to first mixture. Set egg whites aside. Add remaining 1 ½ cups of milk. Cook on medium heat until thick; remove from heat. Add vanilla and butter; place in pie shell and cool. Beat egg whites; when stiffened add 4 tablespoons of sugar. Mix again and place on pie; bake until slightly brown.

Kim Fowler

$\mathcal{K}$EY LIME PIE

1 ¼ c. graham cracker crumbs	2 cans sweetened condensed milk
¼ c. sugar	½ c. Egg Beaters
1/3 c. melted butter	½ c. bottled Key lime juice
	whipped topping

Mix graham cracker crumbs, sugar and melted butter in pie pan. Press mixture firmly onto the bottom and sides of the pan. Combine sweetened condensed milk, Egg Beaters and lime juice in bowl. Whisk together until thoroughly combined. Pour filling into crust. Bake at 350° for 20 minutes. Chill at least 6 hours. Garnish with whipped topping after slicing.

Jodi Sears

$\mathcal{L}$EMON PIE

1 can lemon pie filling	4 Tbsp. lemon juice
1 can sweetened condensed milk	1 graham cracker pie shell
	Cool Whip

Combine first 3 ingredients. Pour in graham cracker crust. Top with Cool Whip. Sprinkle with graham cracker crumbs and garnish with lemon slices.

Kelley Hyde

LINDA SATTERFIELD'S CHOCOLATE CHIP PIE

2 eggs, slightly beaten
1 c. sugar
½ c. butter, melted
1 tsp. vanilla extract
¼ c. cornstarch
1 c. pecans, chopped

1 (6 oz.) pkg. semi-sweet
   chocolate chips
1 (9-inch) pie crust
   (unbaked)
vanilla ice cream (optional)

Combine eggs and sugar. Add butter and vanilla; mix well. Blend in cornstarch. Stir in pecans and chocolate chips. Pour into pie crust. Bake at 350° for 45 to 50 minutes. Serve warm with vanilla ice cream if desired.

Millie Cline

MACAROON PIE

3 egg whites, beaten stiff
1 c. sugar
1 tsp. almond flavoring
12 pecans, chopped fine

12 saltine crackers, crushed
12 dates, chopped fine
whipped cream garnish (if
   desired)

Add sugar, gradually, to beaten egg whites. Mix pecans, cracker crumbs, almond flavoring and dates. Fold mixture into egg white mixture slowly. Gently pour into a greased pie pan or oblong pan and bake at 350° for 30 minutes. Cool, slice and serve with whipped cream.

Mary Johnston
Honorary Member

PECAN PIE

3 eggs
¾ c. brown sugar
½ c. dark corn syrup
½ c. light corn syrup

½ tsp. vanilla
2 Tbsp. melted butter
1 c. chopped pecans
1 unbaked 9-inch pie shell

Beat eggs and add sugar, syrups, vanilla and butter. Stir vigorously. Pour into unbaked 9-inch pie shell and cover with chopped pecans. Bake at 375° for approximately 40 minutes, or until filling is set.

If center is not set but pie edges are getting too brown, can cover edges with foil to keep from overbaking.

Lisa Woodruff

REFRESHING SUMMER PIE

1 pkg. cream cheese, softened
1 small can crushed
  pineapple, drained
½ c. chopped pecans

1 pkg. Dream Whip or small
  container Cool Whip
1 ½ c. powdered sugar
1 Tbsp. vanilla
1 baked pie shell

Whip cream cheese. Add sugar, pineapple, pecans and vanilla. Fold Cool Whip into cream cheese mixture. Pour into pie shell and chill.

Denise Cooper
Honorary Member

SADIE'S COCONUT PIE

2 Tbsp. butter
¾ c. sugar
⅛ tsp. salt
⅓ c. all-purpose flour
2 eggs, beaten
2 c. milk, scalded

½ tsp. vanilla extract
1 (3 ½ oz.) can flaked
  coconut
1 (9-inch) pie crust, baked
Meringue

Combine butter, sugar, salt, flour and eggs. Add milk gradually, stirring constantly. Cook in a double boiler until thick and smooth. Add vanilla and coconut. Pour into pie crust. After adding meringue, bake at 325° for 20 minutes.

Meringue:
4 egg whites
¼ tsp. cream of tartar

⅓ c. sugar

Beat egg whites and cream of tartar until foamy. Gradually beat in sugar. Beat until stiff peaks form. Place on top of pie.

Judy McGarity
Honorary Member

STRAWBERRY PEACH PIE

2 graham cracker crusts
12 oz. cream cheese
1 c. powdered sugar
½ c. chopped pecans

12 oz. Cool Whip
sliced fresh fruit (peaches or
  strawberries)

Mix softened cream cheese, sugar and pecans. Spread in pie crusts. Add sliced fruit. Top with Cool Whip. Chill before serving.

Laura Stanley

Chess Squares

4 eggs
1 cake mix
1 box 10x confectioners sugar

8 oz. cream cheese, softened
½ c. chopped pecans
1 stick margarine

Preheat oven to 350°. Melt margarine in microwave. Combine well the dry cake mix, margarine and 1 egg (slightly beaten). Press mixture into 9 x 13 casserole dish. Press chopped pecans onto bottom layer.

Use electric hand mixer to mix softened cream cheese and 3 eggs (slightly beaten) until smooth and creamy. Add box of confectioners sugar and carefully mix with a spoon. Then use electric mixer to mix until smooth and creamy. Pour this mixture over the bottom layer. Bake for 55 minutes. Cool before cutting. Best at room temperature.

Kim Fowler

Chocolate Peanut Butter Bars

1 (18.25 oz.) pkg. plain yellow
  cake mix
½ c. butter, melted
1 c. creamy peanut butter
2 eggs

1 (12 oz.) pkg. semi-sweet
  chocolate chips
1 (14 oz.) can sweetened
  condensed milk
2 Tbsp. butter
2 tsp. vanilla

Preheat oven to 325°. Combine cake mix, melted butter, peanut butter and eggs in a large bowl using a mixer or spoon. Press this into a 9 x 13 pan, reserving 1 ½ cups of the mixture to crumble on top.

In a small pot, melt chocolate chips, sweetened condensed milk and butter. Remove from heat and stir in the vanilla. Spread chocolate mixture over the mixture pressed in the pan and then drop the 1 ½ cups of reserved cake mixture on top evenly.

Note: This will not completely cover the chocolate mixture and this is okay.

Bake for 20 to 25 minutes. Cool completely before cutting into bars.

Julie Pennington

Fudge Brownies

2 c. sugar
4 eggs
½ c. vegetable oil
1 tsp. vanilla

⅓ c. self-rising flour
½ tsp. salt
10 Tbsp. cocoa

Preheat oven to 350°. Mix all ingredients and pour into a 9 x 13 baking dish. Bake for 20 to 30 minutes, or until done.

Kelley Hyde

$\mathscr{H}$ERSHEY'S SYMPHONY BROWNIES

1 (19.8 oz.) box Betty Crocker
  fudge brownie mix
2 large eggs
¼ c. water

½ c. vegetable oil
2 (7 oz.) Hershey's Symphony
  milk chocolate candy bars

Preheat oven to 350°. Lightly grease the bottom only of a 9 x 13-inch baking pan. Set aside. In a large mixing bowl, prepare brownie mix according to package directions, using 2 eggs, ¼ cup water and ½ cup oil. Stir until smooth. Spread half the batter evenly into prepared pan. Break candy bars into pieces and place them evenly spaced apart on top of batter. Top with remaining brownie batter.

Bake 25 to 30 minutes or until a toothpick inserted near center comes out with a few moist crumbs clinging to it. Remove pan from oven and let cool on wire rack before cutting into squares.

Patti Skelton
Honorary Member

$\mathscr{H}$OMEMADE KIT KAT BARS

75 Club crackers
½ lb. (2 sticks) unsalted
  butter
2 c. graham cracker crumbs
1 c. firmly packed dark
  brown sugar

½ c. milk
⅓ c. granulated sugar
⅔ c. peanut butter
½ c. semi-sweet chocolate
  chips
½ c. butterscotch chips

Line 9 x 13-inch rectangular baking pan with one layer of Club crackers (you may need to break some to fit). Melt butter in large saucepan over medium heat. Add graham cracker crumbs, dark brown sugar, milk and granulated sugar. Bring to a boil. Boil for 5 minutes, stirring constantly. Remove pan from heat. Pour half of the butter mixture over crackers in pan. Smooth surface with spatula. Arrange another layer of Club crackers over butter mixture. Pour remaining butter mixture over surface. Smooth surface with spatula. Arrange third layer of crackers over top.

Combine peanut butter, chocolate chips and butterscotch chips in a small saucepan. Melt over medium-low heat, stirring constantly. Spread evenly over crackers. Cool to room temperature; then cover and refrigerate 2 hours. Cut into 2-inch bars. Bars will keep for 2 weeks stored in an airtight container.

Janet Roach
Honorary Member

$\mathscr{P}$UMPKIN BARS

4 eggs
1 ⅔ c. granulated sugar
1 c. cooking oil
1 (16 oz.) can pumpkin
2 c. all-purpose flour
2 tsp. baking powder

2 tsp. ground cinnamon
1 tsp. salt
1 tsp. baking soda
1 container cream cheese
   frosting*

*Or use recipe for Homemade Cream Cheese Frosting.
Preheat oven to 350°. In mixer bowl, beat together eggs, granulated sugar, oil and pumpkin until light and fluffy. In a separate bowl, stir together flour, baking powder, cinnamon, salt and soda. Add dry mixture to pumpkin mixture a little at a time and mix thoroughly. Spread batter in ungreased 9 x 13-inch or 10 x 15-inch pan. Bake for 30 to 35 minutes. Cool. Frost. Cut into bars.

Homemade Cream Cheese Frosting:

1 (3 oz.) pkg. cream cheese,
   softened
½ c. butter or margarine,
   softened

1 tsp. vanilla
2 c. sifted powdered sugar

Cream together cream cheese and butter or margarine. Stir in vanilla. Add powdered sugar, a little at a time, beating well until mixture is smooth.

Melissa Whatley

$\mathscr{C}$HOCOLATE SNOWFLAKE COOKIES

2 c. sugar
½ c. vegetable oil
4 oz. unsweetened baking
   chocolate, melted
4 eggs

2 tsp. almond or vanilla
   extract (by preference)
2 c. flour
2 tsp. baking powder
½ tsp. salt
¾ c. powdered sugar, sifted

Combine the first 3 ingredients in a large mixing bowl. Beat at medium speed until blended. Add eggs and extract, mixing well. Combine flour, baking powder and salt in separate bowl. Add about ¼ of the mixture at a time to the chocolate mixture, mixing after each addition. Cover and chill dough at least 2 hours.
Shape dough into 1-inch balls and roll in powdered sugar. Place cookies 2-inches apart on a greased cookie sheet. Bake at 350° for 10 minutes. Cool on wire racks. Can be frozen for later use.

Lori Davis

CREAM CHEESE COOKIES

2 sticks butter, softened	**2 c. flour**
1 (3 oz.) pkg. cream cheese	**1 tsp. vanilla**
1 ½ c. sugar	

Preheat oven to 400°. Blend the butter, cream cheese and sugar. Add the flour and vanilla. Drop cookies by rounded teaspoons onto ungreased cookie sheet. Bake for 6 minutes then remove from pan immediately.

Julie Pennington

CRISPY THIN OATMEAL COOKIES

2 c. crushed pecans (can use less or more)	**½ tsp. baking powder**
	½ tsp. salt
2 c. oatmeal (quick oats; uncooked)	**¾ c. cooking oil**
	1 tsp. vanilla flavoring
2 c. sugar	**2 eggs**
8 Tbsp. plain flour	

Mix first 6 ingredients together; then add next 3 ingredients. Mix all together again; then drop by teaspoons on a foil covered cookie baking sheet. Bake at 350° for 15 minutes. Leave space for mixture to spread. Let cool and peel foil from cookies.

Kaye Rogers
Honorary Member

GEORGIA BOWL COOKIES

2 lb. white chocolate	**3 c. crispy rice cereal**
1 c. peanut butter	**1 c. miniature marshmallows**
2 c. peanuts	

Melt chocolate and blend in peanut butter. Stir in nuts, crispy rice cereal and marshmallows. Spoon onto waxed paper; leave until firm. Store in airtight container or in refrigerator, covered.

Cookbook Committee

$\mathscr{L}$EMON DELIGHT COOKIES

1 box lemon cake mix with pudding	1 egg, slightly beaten
2 c. frozen whipped topping, thawed	½ c. confectioners sugar

Preheat oven to 350°. Combine cake mix, whipped topping and egg. Mix until moist. Form into small balls and roll in confectioners sugar and place on baking sheet. Bake for 9 minutes. Remove from baking sheet immediately and place on waxed paper until cool.

Julie Pennington

$\mathscr{M}$EXICAN HOT CHOCOLATE COOKIES

¾ c. packed dark brown sugar	1 c. all-purpose flour
¼ c. sugar (granulated)	1 tsp. baking soda
2 large eggs (at room temperature)	½ tsp. salt
1 Tbsp. vegetable oil	6 Tbsp. unsweetened cocoa
1 tsp. vanilla extract	½ tsp. cayenne pepper or more to taste
1 Tbsp. unsweetened applesauce	½ tsp. ground cinnamon
	½ c. mini chocolate chips

Beat the sugars and the eggs until thick and pale brown, about 5 minutes. Mix in oil, vanilla and applesauce. Set aside. Mix the dry ingredients (except chocolate chips) together. Gradually stir in dry ingredients until blended. Add chocolate chips and drop by teaspoonfuls onto a greased cookie sheet about 2-inches apart (they will spread quite a bit) and bake at 350° for 10 minutes.

Jory Cannon
Honorary Member

$\mathscr{M}$IMI'S OATMEAL CHOCOLATE CHIP COOKIES

1 c. sugar	3 c. quick oats
1 c. brown sugar	1 ½ c. all-purpose flour
1 c. margarine, softened	1 tsp. baking soda
2 eggs	1 tsp. salt
1 tsp. vanilla	2 c. semi-sweet chocolate chips
2 Tbsp. water	

Cream sugars and margarine together; add eggs and mix. Pour in vanilla and water; then add remaining ingredients. Bake at 350° on greased cookie sheets for 8 to 10 minutes.

Lisa Woodruff

MINT CHOCOLATE CHIP COOKIES

1 pouch (1 lb. 1.5 oz.) sugar
  cookie mix
½ c. butter, softened
½ tsp. mint extract
6 to 8 drops of green food
  coloring
1 egg
1 c. crème de menthe baking
  chips
1 c. semi-sweet chocolate
  chips

Preheat oven to 350°. In a large bowl, stir first 5 ingredients together until a soft dough forms. Stir in crème de menthe chips and semi-sweet chips. Using a small cookie scoop or teaspoon, drop dough 2-inches apart onto an ungreased cookie sheet. Bake 8 to 10 minutes. Cool completely.

Emily Jobe

NATURAL CEREAL COOKIES

½ c. vegetable shortening
1 c. firmly packed brown
  sugar
1 egg
3 Tbsp. milk
1 tsp. vanilla
1 ¼ c. all-purpose flour
½ tsp. soda
¼ tsp. salt
2 c. granola natural cereal
  (raisin and date or other
  preferred mixture)

Beat together shortening and sugar until light and fluffy. Blend in egg, milk and vanilla. Add combined flour, soda and salt. Mix well. Stir in cereal. Drop by rounded teaspoons onto greased cookie sheet. Bake at 350° for 10 to 12 minutes.

Anita Geoghagan
Honorary Member

ORANGE BALL COOKIES

1 lb. vanilla wafers, crushed
1 lb. powdered sugar
1 (6 oz.) frozen orange juice,
  thawed
¼ lb. soft margarine
½ c. chopped nuts
flaked coconut

Mix vanilla wafers, powdered sugar, orange juice, margarine and nuts. Roll into small balls. Roll in coconut. Store in airtight container in refrigerator.

Mary Johnston
Honorary Member

*R*ED VELVET COOKIES

1 (8 oz.) cream cheese (room
  temperature)
½ c. butter, softened
1 tsp. vanilla

1 (18 oz.) box red velvet cake
  mix
powdered sugar (for rolling
  or dusting)

In a large bowl, with an electric mixer, cream the cream cheese and butter until smooth. Beat in egg, then the vanilla. Beat in the cake mix. Cover and refrigerate for 2 hours to firm up.

After refrigerating the cream cheese mixture, preheat oven to 350°. Roll batter into tablespoon sized balls and then roll them in powdered sugar. Place on ungreased cookie sheet, 2-inches apart. Bake 12 minutes. The cookies will remain soft and "gooey." Cool completely and sprinkle with more confectioners sugar, if desired.

Julie Pennington

*T*RAIL COOKIES

3 eggs
1 ¼ c. packed light brown
  sugar
1 c. granulated sugar
½ tsp. salt
½ tsp. vanilla extract
1 (12 oz.) jar creamy peanut
  butter

1 stick butter, softened
½ c. M&M's
½ c. chocolate chips (jumbo
  are best)
¼ c. raisins (optional)
2 tsp. baking soda
4 ½ c. quick cooking oatmeal
  (not instant)

Preheat the oven to 350°F. Line cookie sheets with parchment paper. In a large mixing bowl or stand mixer, combine the eggs and sugars until mixed well. Add the salt, vanilla, peanut butter and butter. Mix well. Stir in the chocolate candies, chocolate chips, raisins, baking soda and oatmeal. Drop by tablespoons 2-inches apart onto the prepared cookie sheets. Bake for 8 to 10 minutes. Let stand about 3 minutes before transferring to wire racks to cool. When cool, store in airtight containers.

Bonny Spears

$\mathcal{W}$HITE CHOCOLATE CHIP MACADAMIA NUT
COOKIES

1 c. margarine, softened
1 c. firmly packed brown
  sugar
1 c. sugar
2 large eggs
2 tsp. vanilla
3 c. all-purpose flour
1 tsp. baking soda

1 tsp. baking powder
1 tsp. salt
1 ½ c. quick oats
2 c. (12 oz.) white chocolate
  morsels
1 c. coarsely chopped
  macadamia nuts

Beat margarine at medium speed until creamy; gradually add sugars, beating well. Add eggs, 1 at a time, beating just until yellow disappears. Stir in vanilla. Combine flour, baking soda, baking powder and salt; gradually add to butter mixture until blended. Add oats, morsels and macadamia nuts. Drop by tablespoonfuls onto greased baking sheets. Bake at 350° for 12 minutes.

Lisa Woodruff

$\mathcal{A}$PPLE DUMPLINGS

2 Granny Smith apples,
  peeled and cut into 8 pieces
  each
2 tubes crescent rolls
  (original; 8 to a tube)

1 c. sugar
1 tsp. cinnamon (optional)
1 ½ sticks butter, melted
12 oz. Mountain Dew soft
  drink

Unroll crescent rolls and wrap each triangle around a slice of apple. Place in a 13 x 9-inch dish. Add sugar and cinnamon to melted butter. Stir well. Pour mixture over and around dumplings. Pour Mountain Dew over all. Bake at 325° for 40 to 50 minutes or until golden. Makes 16 servings.

This seems like a very strange combination of ingredients, and I agree! But believe me, it's delicious, especially served warm with vanilla bean ice cream.

Anita Geoghagan
Honorary Member

BREAD PUDDING WITH PRALINE SAUCE

day old French bread dinner
  rolls (or any crusty dinner
  rolls or loaf of bread;
  approximately 8 rolls or 1
  large loaf)
1 c. white sugar

1 qt. half and half
5 eggs
¼ tsp. vanilla extract
Praline Sauce
Optional garnishes: whipped
  cream, walnuts

Cut each roll in half and then cut into ⅜-inch or ½-inch slices. Transfer to a large bowl. Sprinkle sugar over the bread slices. Pour half and half over the bread. In a medium bowl, beat together the eggs and vanilla. Pour over the bread. Mix all ingredients gently but thoroughly; then let mixture soak for 15 minutes. Mix again and then allow to soak another 15 minutes.

Preheat oven to 350°. Spread the bread mixture evenly in a lightly greased 9 x 13-inch baking dish. Bake for 45 to 50 minutes, until pudding is set and lightly browned on top. Serve each piece with 2 to 3 tablespoons Praline Sauce and optional whipped cream and chopped walnuts.

Praline Sauce:

½ c. (1 stick) unsalted butter
½ lb. (1 ⅛ c.) light brown
  sugar

1 c. heavy whipping cream
¼ tsp. vanilla extract

In a heavy saucepan, melt the butter over medium-high heat. Stir in the brown sugar; then bring to a rolling boil. Boil for 2 minutes. Stir in the cream. Return to a boil; then immediately remove from the heat. Stir in the vanilla. Serve at room temperature.

Anita Geoghagan
Honorary Member

CHOCOLATE COBBLER

1 c. self-rising flour
6 Tbsp. butter
¾ c. white sugar

2 Tbsp. unsweetened cocoa
 powder
½ c. milk
1 tsp. vanilla extract

Topping:
½ to ¾ c. brown sugar
¼ c. white sugar
¼ c. cocoa

1 ½ c. hot tap water
1 c. chopped pecans
(optional)

Preheat oven to 350°. In an 8 x 8 baking dish, add 6 tablespoons of butter to the pan. (The butter does not have to be cut up.) Place the dish into your preheated oven. This will let the butter melt while you mix up the rest of the ingredients.

In a separate bowl, add self-rising flour, ¾ cup of white sugar and 2 tablespoons of cocoa powder. Stir the dry ingredients together. Next add to the dry ingredients ½ cup milk and 1 teaspoon vanilla extract. Stir together well.

Remove your butter pan from the oven and add the chocolate mixture to the dish of melted butter. The chocolate batter tends to be a bit thick and pretty difficult to spread out evenly, but spread as best you can. In a small bowl, add in ½ cup brown sugar, ¼ cup of white sugar and ¼ cup of cocoa powder. Mix well. Sprinkle the topping evenly over the top of the chocolate mixture. Get 1 ½ cups of very hot water. The water can be heated up in the microwave. Slowly pour the hot water over the top of the cobbler. Place the dish in the oven for about 30 to 35 minutes. Let cool and serve warm with vanilla ice cream.

Laura Stanley

MARY LOU'S APPLE DUMPLINGS

1 can crescent rolls
1 Granny Smith apple
1 stick butter

¾ c. brown sugar
½ tsp. cinnamon
¾ c. Mountain Dew

Grease a 9 x 13 dish. Preheat oven to 350°. Cut apple into 8 slices. Roll each slice in a crescent roll. Cook butter, brown sugar and cinnamon in a saucepan. Pour in the Mountain Dew. Pour mixture over apple rolls and bake at 350° covered for 15 minutes; then uncovered at 350° for 15 minutes.

Julie Pennington

ℱRUIT COBBLER

1 stick margarine	1 c. milk
1 c. self-rising flour	3 c. fruit (fresh or frozen;
1 c. sugar	peaches, blueberries, etc.)

Melt margarine in a baking dish. In a bowl, mix flour, sugar and milk. Pour into margarine; don't stir. Pour fruit evenly over the flour mixture; don't stir. Bake until brown, approximately 45 minutes at 350°.

Ashley Rusbridge

𝒢RANDMOTHER KING'S RICE PUDDING

1 c. rice	½ c. butter
1 ½ c. sugar	egg yolks (reserve whites for
2 large eggs	meringue)
1 tsp. nutmeg	salt to taste

Boil rice until done. Combine all ingredients together in a buttered baking dish. Cook until browned in a 325° oven.

Meringue:

2 egg whites	4 Tbsp. sugar

Beat egg whites until firm. Add sugar. Spread over rice mixture. Bake at 450° just until browned.

Angie Hathcock

𝒫EACH ENCHILADAS

2 cans refrigerated crescent	1 c. butter, melted
rolls	1 tsp. cinnamon
4 fresh large peaches,	1 (12 oz.) citrus flavored soft
quartered	drink (Mello Yello)
1 ½ c. sugar	

Preheat oven to 350°. Separate rolls into triangles. Roll up around quartered peach starting at wide end. Place point side down on lightly greased 13 x 9 baking dish. Stir together sugar, melted butter and cinnamon. Drizzle over rolls. Pour soft drink over rolls. Bake 35 to 45 minutes until golden brown and bubbly.

Jamie Morgan
Honorary Member

APLE CREAM TARTS

Sugar Mixture:
1 ½ c. brown sugar   ¼ c. butter
½ c. maple flavored syrup

Filling Mixture:
1 (8 oz.) pkg. cream cheese,   ¼ c. powdered sugar
  softened   2 Tbsp. butter, softened

Dough:
2 (10 oz.) cans refrigerated flaky biscuits

Preheat oven to 350°. In a medium saucepan, combine the Sugar Mixture. Melt thoroughly and pour into an ungreased 9 x 13 pan. In a small bowl, combine the Filling Mixture. Separate the biscuits and roll each one into approximately a 4-inch circle. Spoon 1 tablespoon of the filling into the middle of each biscuit. Overlap the sides of the dough over the filling, forming finger shaped rolls. Arrange the rolls, seam side down, in 2 rows of 10 biscuits each over the sugar mixture. Bake at 350° for 25 to 30 minutes or until deep golden brown. Cool 3 to 5 minutes and serve.

Julie Pennington

$\mathcal{C}$HOCOLATE CHIP CHEESE DIP

2 (8 oz.) cream cheese,   ¼ c. brown sugar
  softened   1 tsp. vanilla
1 c. butter, softened   1 bag mini chocolate chips
½ c. powdered sugar

Mix the first 5 ingredients together with a mixer. Stir in the chocolate chips. Place in serving bowl or roll into a ball. Chill until cold and set. Serve with graham cracker sticks.

Julie Pennington

Chocolate Éclair Dessert

1 (16 oz.) pkg. graham
   crackers
2 (4 oz.) pkg. vanilla
   pudding

3 c. milk
1 (8 oz.) carton Cool Whip
1 (8 oz.) pkg. cream cheese
1 can milk chocolate frosting

Prepare pudding mix with 3 cups milk. Beat cream cheese until soft and blend in the Cool Whip. Fold in the prepared pudding.

Place 1 layer of graham crackers in a 9 x 13 dish. Layer ½ of the pudding mixture on top of the graham crackers, another layer of graham crackers, then the remaining pudding and then the final layer of graham crackers. Remove the plastic lid and foil from the cake icing. Microwave for 1 minute; stir well and spread onto layer of the graham crackers. Chill well before serving.

Julie Pennington

Chocolate Passion Bowl

1 baked 9-inch square
   brownie layer, cooled and
   cut into 1-inch cubes
   (about 5 ½ c.)
3 c. cold milk

2 pkg. (4 serving size each)
   chocolate flavored instant
   pudding and pie filling
1 (8 oz.) tub whipped
   topping, thawed and
   divided
1 pt. (2 c.) raspberries

Pour milk into large bowl. Add dry pudding mixes. Beat with wire whisk 2 minutes or until well blended. Gently stir in 1 cup of the whipped topping.

Place half of the brownie cubes in 2-quart serving bowl (preferably glass trifle bowl). Top with layers of half of each of the pudding mixture, remaining whipped topping and raspberries. Repeat all layers. Refrigerate at least 1 hour before serving. Store leftovers in refrigerator.

Millie Cline

DOUBLE CHOCOLATE MOCHA TRIFLE

1 pkg. brownie mix, cooked
   according to pkg.
   directions
1 ¾ c. cold milk
2 pkg. white chocolate
   instant pudding mix
¼ c. warm water
2 tsp. instant coffee granules
2 tubs Cool Whip, thawed
4 to 6 Heath bars, chopped

Make brownies according to package directions, or you can purchase brownie bites already made from the store to save time. Mix pudding and milk until thickened. Dissolve coffee granules in warm water and add to pudding mixture; mix well. Fold in Cool Whip. Cut up brownies into 1-inch pieces. Chop up Heath bars. Layer first with the pudding mixture, then brownies and Heath bar. Repeat in order until trifle bowl is full. Refrigerate.

Lori Davis

OREO CHEESECAKE MINIS

42 Oreos (30 whole and 12
   coarsely chopped)
2 lb. cream cheese (room
   temperature)
1 c. sugar
1 tsp. vanilla extract
4 large eggs (room
   temperature), lightly
   beaten
1 c. sour cream
⅛ tsp. salt

Preheat oven to 275°. Line muffin tins with paper liners. Put 1 whole cookie in the bottom of each liner. Beat cream cheese with electric mixer until smooth. Gradually add sugar; beat until combined and add vanilla. Slowly add eggs and beat until mixed. Beat in sour cream and salt. Stir in chopped cookies by hand.

Divide batter evenly among paper liners; fill each one almost to the top. Bake approximately 22 minutes, or until filling is set. Outsides should be stiff, but the centers can be a little wiggly. Transfer to a wire rack. Cool completely. Refrigerate uncovered for 4 hours.

Melissa Auringer

OREO ICE CREAM DESSERT

24 Oreo cookies, crushed
½ c. butter, melted
½ gal. vanilla ice cream, softened
1 (4 oz.) German chocolate bar
½ c. butter

⅔ c. sugar
⅔ c. evaporated milk or half and half
1 tsp. vanilla
⅛ tsp. salt
1 (8 oz.) container frozen whipped topping, thawed

Combine cookies and melted butter and place in a 9 x 13-inch pan. Spread softened ice cream over crust and freeze.

Combine the next 6 ingredients and boil for 4 minutes. Cool and pour over top of ice cream. Freeze for about 30 minutes. Top with container of frozen whipped topping and freeze. Can sprinkle chopped nuts or additional crushed cookies on top. Makes 10 to 12 servings.

Wanda Roach
Honorary Member

INDIVIDUAL BANANA PUDDINGS

½ c. firmly packed light brown sugar
¼ c. butter
4 large ripe bananas, sliced
1 c. granulated sugar, divided

⅓ c. all-purpose flour
2 large eggs
2 c. milk
4 large eggs, separated
2 tsp. vanilla extract
48 vanilla wafers

Cook brown sugar and butter in a large skillet over medium heat, stirring constantly, 2 to 3 minutes or until bubbly. Add bananas; cook 2 minutes or until thoroughly heated. Remove from heat. Whisk together ¾ cup granulated sugar, next 3 ingredients and 4 egg yolks in a heavy saucepan. Cook over medium-low heat, whisking constantly, 8 to 10 minutes or until a pudding like thickness. Mixture will just begin to bubble and will hold soft peaks when whisk is lifted. Remove from heat and stir in vanilla.

Divide half of banana mixture, pudding and wafers among 8 (1-cup) ramekins or ovenproof glass dishes. Layer with remaining banana mixture, pudding and vanilla wafers. Beat 4 egg whites at high speed with an electric mixer until foamy. Add remaining ¼ cup granulated sugar, 1 tablespoon at a time, beating until stiff peaks form and sugar dissolves (2 to 4 minutes). Spread meringue over ramekins. Place ramekins on a baking sheet. Bake at 325° for 15 to 20 minutes or until meringue is golden. Let cool on a wire rack 30 minutes.

Rebecca Johnston
Honorary Member

NO-COOK BANANA PUDDING

3 c. cold water
2 large boxes instant vanilla
  pudding (unprepared)
3 cans condensed milk

2 large (16 oz.) containers
  sour cream
2 large containers Cool Whip
8 ripe bananas
2 boxes vanilla wafers

Combine water and pudding in a large mixing bowl. Add condensed milk and sour cream. Mix well. Fold in Cool Whip until color is consistent throughout. Use vanilla wafers, sliced bananas and pudding mixture to layer into a very large bowl. Cover and refrigerate before serving.

Melissa Whatley

ANGIE'S CARAMEL POPCORN

2 bags microwave (light or plain) popcorn

Pop popcorn. Pour onto 2 foil lined baking sheets. Pick out kernels.

Toffee:
1 stick butter   10 marshmallows
½ c. sugar

Make Toffee in saucepan on low heat. Melt together ingredients. Pour Toffee on top of 2 trays of popped popcorn. Toss lightly. Bake at 225° to 250° for 20 minutes. Stir at 10 minutes. Turn out onto lined cookie sheets or tray. Cool. Store in an airtight container. Makes great gifts!

Bonny Spears

$\mathcal{B}$RANDIED FRUIT

First Day:

¼ c. apricot or peach brandy
1 pkg. dry yeast
1 c. canned peaches, drained

½ c. maraschino cherries,
  drained
1 c. sugar

Pour ingredients into glass container and cover loosely. (Wait exactly one week to add next ingredients.)

Week 2:

1 c. canned diced pineapple,
  drained
1 c. sugar

¼ c. maraschino cherries,
  drained

Stir well.

Third Week:

1 c. canned pears or apricots,
  drained
1 c. sugar

¼ c. maraschino cherries,
  drained

Stir well.
Great served by itself or over pound cake or vanilla ice cream.

Becky Buice
Honorary Member

$\mathcal{C}$HOCOLATE COOKIE BARK

1 pkg. (8 sq.) Baker's
  semi-sweet baking
  chocolate
1 pkg. (6 sq.) Baker's
  premium white baking
  chocolate

2 Tbsp. peanut butter
10 Oreo chocolate sandwich
  cookies

Put semi-sweet and white chocolate in separate bowls. Microwave until melted. Put peanut butter in white chocolate and mix crumbled Oreo cookies in each bowl; mix. Drop spoonfuls of the chocolate mixtures next to/on top of each other onto wax paper on a baking sheet (or alternating lines). Cut through mixtures several times with knife for marble effect. Refrigerate at least 1 hour or until firm. Break into pieces and enjoy.

Michelle Bowden

COBWEB CANDY

1 c. chocolate chips
2 Tbsp. butter
1/8 c. milk (or just enough to
  dissolve sugar)

1 1/2 c. powdered sugar
3 c. mini marshmallows

Combine chocolate chips and butter in medium bowl. Microwave 2 to 4 minutes or until chips can be stirred smooth. Combine milk and powdered sugar in small bowl; add to chocolate mixture. Stir in marshmallows until well coated. Pour onto wax paper; divide mixture in half. Form each half into 9-inch long log (like a roll of cookie dough). Refrigerate; slice into rounds when ready to serve. Makes 36 slices.

Melissa Whatley

GELATIN STRAWBERRIES

1 (15 oz.) can sweetened
  condensed milk
1 lb. fine coconut

2 (3 oz.) pkg. strawberry
  flavored gelatin
1 tsp. vanilla extract
1/2 tsp. almond extract

Mix condensed milk, coconut, 1 package of dry gelatin and flavorings. When well mixed, roll into small balls and then roll in remaining package of gelatin to coat thoroughly. Allow to dry before storing in airtight container.

Recipe may be varied by using other flavored gelatin like orange or lemon. Store in the refrigerator in airtight lidded container. Take out 1 hour before serving. Great for tea parties.

Mary Johnston
Honorary Member

PEANUT BUTTER BALLS

1 lb. butter (at room
  temperature)
1 medium (28 oz.) jar creamy
  Jif peanut butter

2 1/2 boxes powdered sugar
1 bag chocolate wafers
1/2 bag mini chocolate chips

Cream butter until light and fluffy. Add peanut butter and cream together. Stir in the sugar. Mix by hand until smooth. Shape with hands into balls and refrigerate overnight. Melt the chocolate wafers and chips in a double boiler. Coat the chilled balls with chocolate.

Julie Pennington

$\mathcal{P}$ENUCHE

| 1 box light brown sugar | 2 Tbsp. butter or margarine |
| 3⁄4 c. milk | 1 tsp. vanilla flavoring |

Heat sugar, milk and butter over medium heat, stirring until sugar melts. Lower heat and cook, without stirring, to soft-ball stage (240°). Remove from heat and add vanilla. Cool to room temperature. Beat constantly until thick and pour into buttered glass dish. Store in airtight container in the refrigerator.

Becky Buice
Honorary Member

$\mathcal{S}$ALTED TOFFEE BARK

1 sleeve saltine crackers	1 (12 oz.) pkg. semi-sweet
2 sticks butter	chocolate morsels
1 c. brown sugar	sea salt

Preheat oven to 400°. Line a larger baking sheet with aluminum foil and place the saltine crackers, sides touching each other, in a rectangle shape on the foil. Turn sides of the foil up close to the crackers to form a container.

Melt the butter with the brown sugar and bring to a boil for 3 minutes. Carefully pour the mixture over the crackers, being careful not to move them. Bake for 7 minutes. Remove from oven and sprinkle chocolate morsels evenly over the hot crackers. Let the chocolate melt by itself and then gently spread it around. Sprinkle the chocolate melted mixture with a small amount of sea salt. Refrigerate to chill until firm. Remove from the pan and foil and break into pieces.

Variations: Use 1⁄2 bag of semi-sweet and 1⁄2 bag of milk chocolate morsels mixed together. In addition to the 1 bag of semi-sweet chocolate morsels, add in 1⁄2 bag of butterscotch chips. Sprinkle nuts of your preference on top of melted chocolate. When mixture is partially cooled, but not firm, sprinkle mini chocolate candies on top.

Julie Pennington

$\mathcal{C}$ANDIED PECANS

1 1⁄2 c. sugar	1⁄4 tsp. vanilla
1⁄2 c. milk	2 1⁄2 c. pecans
1 tsp. Karo light corn syrup	

In a 2-quart saucepan, mix first 3 ingredients. Cook to soft-ball stage (238° on a candy thermometer). Add pecans and vanilla and stir until creamy. Quickly turn out onto wax paper and separate.

Ashley Rusbridge

$\mathcal{C}$INNAMON SUGAR ALMONDS

1 ½ c. sugar	1 egg white
1 ½ c. brown sugar	2 tsp. vanilla
3 Tbsp. cinnamon	3 c. almonds
⅛ tsp. salt	¼ c. water

In a medium sized bowl, mix together sugars, cinnamon and salt. Set aside. In another medium sized bowl, whisk the egg white and vanilla until it's a little frothy. Add almonds. Make sure the almonds are thoroughly coated in the egg white mixture. Add cinnamon mixture to the almonds and toss until coated.

Thoroughly spray with Pam the stoneware of your crock-pot. Add the divine mixture of almonds and sugar to the crock-pot and turn it to low. Cook 3 to 4 hours, stirring every 30 minutes (I only did 3 hours). In the last hour, add the ¼ cup of water and stir well. This ensures a crunchy yummy coating. Continue to cook the nuts for another 45 minutes to an hour. You have to stir really well, especially as it gets later in the cooking process.

Line a baking sheet with parchment and spread the almonds flat to cool. The almonds will be sticky at this point, so make sure you separate them a little and have no large mounds.

Amanda Locke

$\mathcal{D}$IVINE PECANS

1 lb. pecans	1 c. sugar
2 egg whites	1 stick butter
pinch of salt	

Bake pecans 5 to 10 minutes at 325°. Meanwhile, beat together egg whites, pinch of salt and sugar. Add pecans. Melt butter in 13 x 9 dish. Add pecan mixture and stir to coat. Bake 30 minutes, stirring every 10 minutes. Store cooled nuts in tightly sealed container. Great on salads or as a snack!

JoAnne Knieriem

TRIPLE CHOCOLATE NUT CLUSTERS

1 (16 oz.) jar dry roasted
  peanuts
1 (9.75 oz.) can salted whole
  cashews
2 c. pecan pieces
18 (2 oz.) chocolate bark
  coating squares

1 (12 oz.) pkg. semi-sweet
  chocolate morsels
4 (1 oz.) bittersweet chocolate
  baking squares, broken
  into pieces
1 Tbsp. shortening
1 tsp. vanilla extract

Combine the first 7 ingredients in a slow cooker and cover and cook on low for 2 hours or until chocolate is melted. Stir chocolate and nuts and add vanilla, stirring well to coat.

Drop candy by heaping teaspoonfuls onto wax paper. Let stand at least 2 hours or until firm. Store in an airtight container.

Emily Jobe

beverages

Microwave

& misc.

Helpful Cooking Hints

Frozen gravies or sauces may be a little thicker after thawing than when they were freshly made. Adding a little appropriate liquid - milk, broth, or bouillon - will thin them to the desired consistency.

For extra juicy, extra nutritious hamburgers, add 1/4 cup evaporated milk per pound of meat before shaping.

To ripen green pears, just place 2 or 3 in a brown bag, loosely closed, and store at room temperature out of direct sunlight.

In making pickles, use white vinegar to make clear pickles and coarse salt which comes in 5 pound bags. This is not rock salt. Avoid using iodized salt for pickle making. Most pickles are better if allowed to stand six weeks before using.

Lemon gelatin dissolved in 2 cups of hot apricot nectar with 1 teaspoon of grated lemon added for zip makes a perfect base for jellied fruit salad.

Put a tablespoon of butter in the water when cooking rice, dried beans, macaroni, to keep it from boiling over. Always run cold water over it when done to get the starch out. Reheat over hot water, if necessary.

Never put a cover on anything that is cooked in milk unless you want to spend hours cleaning up the stove when it boils over.

Anything that grows under the ground, start off in cold water - potatoes, beets, carrots, etc. Anything that grows above ground, start off in boiling water - English peas, greens, beans, etc.

To clean aluminum pots when they are stained dark, merely boil with a little cream of tartar, vinegar or acid foods.

Baking powder will remove tea or coffee stains from china pots or cups.

Canned cream soups make excellent sauces for vegetables, fish, etc. Celery with lobster, black bean or onion with cauliflower, tomato with lamb chops.

Slip your hand inside a waxed sandwich bag and you have a perfect mitt for greasing your baking pans and casserole dishes.

To reheat roast, wrap in aluminum foil and heat in a slow oven.

Hard boiled eggs will peel easily if cracked and placed in cold water immediately after taking out of the hot water.

You can cut a meringue pie cleanly by coating both sides of the knife lightly with butter.

When recipe calls for adding raw eggs to hot mixture, always begin by slowly adding a small amount of hot mixture to the beaten eggs to avoid curdling.

To remove fish odor from hands, utensils and dish cloths, use one teaspoon baking soda to quart of water.

To keep icings moist and to prevent cracking, add a pinch of baking soda to the icing.

If soup tastes very salty, a raw piece of potato placed in the pot will absorb the salt.

Pour water into mold and then drain before pouring in mixture to be chilled. Will come out of mold easier.

When rolling cookie dough, sprinkle board with powdered sugar instead of flour. Too much flour makes the dough heavy. When freezing cookies with a frosting, place them in freezer unwrapped for about 2 hours - then wrap without worrying about them sticking together.

BEVERAGES, MICROWAVE & MISCELLANEOUS

$\mathscr{B}$OURBON SLUSH

1 c. sugar
1 (12 oz.) can frozen
lemonade concentrate,
thawed

1 (6 oz.) can frozen orange
juice concentrate, thawed
2 liter lemon lime soda
6 c. water
¾ c. bourbon

Mix together all ingredients except the lemon lime soda. Freeze 2 hours and then stir. Freeze again for 4 hours. Shave off the desired amount to partially fill a glass. Fill the remainder of glass with lemon lime soda.

Julie Pennington

$\mathscr{C}$HAMPAGNE PUNCH

2 bottles champagne (dry or
extra dry variety tastes
best)
1 bottle Sauterne wine

12 oz. lemonade concentrate
1 to 2 liters ginger ale
1 (64 oz.) can pineapple juice

Mix and serve. Make an ice ring of pineapple juice and ginger ale to float in bowl.

Anita Geoghagan
Honorary Member

$\mathscr{C}$HRISTMAS PUNCH

2 (12 oz.) cans pink
lemonade concentrate
1 (12 oz.) can orange juice
concentrate
1 (16 oz.) frozen sliced
strawberries, thawed

1 (2 liter) bottle ginger ale
(diet or regular)
36 oz. water (3 cans)
red food coloring (as desired)

Stir all the ingredients in a large punch bowl. Add ice or an ice ring to keep punch chilled.

Hillary Hall

COFFEE PUNCH

2 Tbsp. instant coffee
½ gal. chocolate milk (do not use 2%)

½ gal. Breyers vanilla ice cream, softened
½ tsp. almond extract

Add the instant coffee to 1 cup of the chocolate milk and stir. Let this mixture sit overnight in the refrigerator prior to using.

Remove the ice cream from the freezer and let it soften. Add the rest of the gallon of chocolate milk, the almond extract and the mixture of chocolate milk and instant coffee.

This recipe serves 12. To double the recipe, we recommend that you use 2 separate mixtures of the chocolate milk and instant coffee.

Kim Fowler

KAREN'S CREAMY CROCK-POT HOT CHOCOLATE

1 ½ c. heavy cream
1 can sweetened condensed milk (14 oz.)

2 c. milk chocolate chocolate chips
1 tsp. vanilla

Add all ingredients to crock-pot. Serve when hot.

Karen McClellan
Honorary Member

ORANGE APPLE CIDER

1 gal. apple cider
3 cinnamon sticks
peel of 1 orange
¼ tsp. nutmeg

additional oranges and cinnamon sticks for garnish (if desired)

Place all ingredients in a slow cooker. Heat, covered, on high for 1 hour. Reduce heat to low until cider is heated through. Remove orange peel before serving. Garnish each serving with orange slices and a cinnamon stick.

Bonny Spears

$\mathscr{P}$ARTY PUNCH

2 (12 oz. each) cans frozen
   grape juice concentrate,
   thawed
1 (12 oz.) can frozen fruit
   punch concentrate, thawed

4 (2 liters) 7-Up or other
   citrus soda
½ gal. raspberry sherbet

Put ½ the sherbet in a decorative punch bowl. Add 1 can grape juice concentrate and ½ can of fruit punch concentrate and 2 of the bottles of soda. Mix together gently without totally dissolving the sherbet. As event progresses, add the remaining ingredients to freshen up the punch bowl.

Bonny Spears

$\mathscr{P}$INA COLADA

1 c. pineapple juice
6 Tbsp. crushed canned
   pineapple (can substitute ½
   c. fresh pineapple; even
   tastier)

5 ½ Tbsp. Coco Lopez cream
   of coconut
2 to 3 tsp. frozen limeade
2 Tbsp. Karo syrup
¾ to 1 c. rum (can also use
   coconut flavored rum)

Mix all ingredients together in blender with crushed ice!

Wendy Landry

$\mathscr{P}$INK PANTY PULL DOWN

4 cans Fresca
1 can pink lemonade frozen
   concentrate

1 can vodka

Mix and serve over ice.

Jana Anderman

$\mathscr{S}$ANDRA'S SAVANNAH SPLASH

2 oz. Capt Morgan rum
2 oz. Malibu rum (coconut
   flavor)

1 oz. crème de banana
   (DeKuyper makes the best)
6 oz. orange juice
1 tsp. grenadine

Shake well. Serve in a tall glass on ice.

Bonny Spears

SLUSH PUNCH

1 pkg. cherry Kool-Aid
  (unsweetened)
1 pkg. powdered pink
  lemonade
4 c. water, brought to boil

1 (12 oz.) can frozen orange
  juice, thawed, with 3 cans
  water (total of 48 oz.)
1 (46 oz.) can pineapple juice
1 to 2 liters Sprite

Bring the 4 cups of water to a boil. Stir in the powdered drink mixes; stir until dissolved. Add the thawed orange juice concentrate, 3 cans of water and the pineapple juice. Stir well. Pour into a freezable container and freeze overnight.

Remove from freezer and spoon out into a punch bowl. Add Sprite.

To make an ADULT version of this, add 1 cup (or more to your taste) of vodka to the juice mix before placing in the freezer.

Julie Pennington

STRAWBERRY PUNCH

2 c. sugar
6 c. water
½ c. lemon juice
2 ½ c. orange juice
4 c. unsweetened pineapple
  juice

2 (10 oz.) pkg. frozen
  strawberries with juice,
  thawed
1 (64 oz.) Sprite

In saucepan over medium heat, combine sugar and water. Simmer, stirring occasionally, until sugar dissolves, about 2 minutes. Cool to room temperature and add orange juice, lemon juice, pineapple juice and strawberries with their juice. Pour mixture into shallow container and freeze.

Remove 1 hour prior to serving. Break into chunks in punch bowl and add lemon lime soda and stir until slushy.

Anne Burke

THE BEST PUNCH

1 (2 liter) bottle ginger ale
1 (46 oz.) can pineapple juice

1 (12 oz.) can frozen
  lemonade concentrate

Mix all ingredients and serve.

If desire a sweeter punch, substitute orange juice concentrate for half the lemonade concentrate. If desired, make an ice ring beforehand from frozen pineapple juice and use it in the punch. Lemon or orange slices may be suspended in the ring for additional decoration.

Anita Geoghagan
Honorary Member

$\mathscr{W}$ASSAIL

4 c. apple cider
1 lemon, sliced
5 cinnamon sticks
1 tsp. whole cloves

4 c. red wine
4 c. orange juice
½ c. sugar

Mix cider, lemon, cinnamon and cloves in a large pot and cook over medium heat for 20 minutes. Add wine, orange juice and sugar and cook until heated through. Remove lemon, cinnamon and cloves before serving.

Barbara Jacoby

$\mathscr{W}$HITE HOT CHOCOLATE

1 gal. whole milk
1 pt. heavy whipping cream
1 c. sugar

2 bags white chocolate chips
2 to 3 tsp. vanilla

Mix and place in crock-pot on high, stirring occasionally, until heated. Turn to low to keep warm.

Wanda Roach
Honorary Member

$\mathscr{M}$ICROWAVE PEANUT BRITTLE

1 c. granulated sugar
½ c. light corn syrup
¼ tsp. salt
1 tsp. vanilla

1 tsp. butter
1 tsp. baking soda
1 c. raw peanuts

In a 2-quart glass dish or bowl, combine sugar, syrup and salt; cover and microwave on High for 4 minutes. Add peanuts and stir; cover and microwave on High for another 4 minutes. Stir in vanilla and butter. Add baking soda and stir quickly; pour onto greased cookie sheet or silicone mat and spread evenly. Allow to cool; then break into pieces.

Lori Davis

$\mathscr{P}$EANUT BUTTER FUDGE

1 c. peanut butter
1 c. butter

1 tsp. vanilla
1 (16 oz.) box powdered sugar

Melt peanut butter and butter together. Add vanilla. Stir in sugar. Mix well. Spread evenly onto 2 greased dinner plates. Wrap and refrigerate. Cut into squares.

Cookbook Committee

$\mathcal{B}$BQ DRY RUB

1 ¼ c. white sugar
1 ¼ c. brown sugar
½ c. salt

¼ c. black pepper
¼ c. paprika

Mix and rub on pork before grilling. Stores well.

Anita Geoghagan
Honorary Member

$\mathcal{B}$LUEBERRY PEPPER JELLY

5 c. blueberries
½ c. lemon juice, divided into
   2 (¼ c.) portions
1 ½ c. water
1 c. jalapeno pepper, seeded
   and chopped fine
2 Tbsp. bell peppers, chopped
   fine

½ c. vinegar
5 c. sugar (you can use ½
   sugar and ½ Splenda also,
   but not just Splenda)
1 (4 oz.) box pectin (low
   sugar formula)

In one saucepan, combine the peppers, vinegar, ¼ cup lemon juice and 1 cup water. Cook on medium-high for 20 minutes; then using a sieve, remove all the peppers from the liquid and set aside. In another saucepan, place blueberries, ¼ cup lemon juice and ½ cup water and cook on medium-high for 20 minutes. Strain with a cheesecloth or jelly bag.

Combine both liquids into one of the pans, adding sugar/Splenda. Cook on medium-low until the sugar dissolves. Skim any foam off of the surface. Bring mix to a boil and add 1 box pectin and bring to a rolling boil for 1 minute. Remove from heat, skim off any foam and ladle into sterilized jelly jars and place lids tightly on the jars.

Boil in a hot water bath (with 1 to 2-inches of water over the lids) for 5 minutes. Set on counter to cool and to set. Listen for the lids to pop. They could pop anywhere from 2 minutes to 2 hours afterward. If they do not pop, they are not sealed and will need to be refrigerated and used immediately.

Serve with cream cheese and Ritz crackers.

Karen McClellan
Honorary Member

$\mathcal{C}$INNAMON BUTTER

1 stick butter, softened to
   room temperature
¼ c. powdered sugar

¼ c. honey
1 Tbsp. ground cinnamon

Mix all together with hand mixer. Store in refrigerator in sealed container.

Bonny Spears

$\mathcal{H}$ORNSBY'S MEAT MARINADE

½ c. olive oil
4 Tbsp. soy sauce
4 Tbsp. lemon juice
2 tsp. garlic powder

1 tsp. black pepper
1 ½ tsp. celery salt
4 Tbsp. finely minced onion

Mix all together. Meat can marinate anywhere from 2 hours to 12 hours (longer is better). GREAT on any type of grilled meat!

Bonny Spears

$\mathcal{H}$APPINESS

2 heaping spoons of patience
1 heart full of love
2 hands full of generosity

a dash of laughter
1 head full of understanding

Add to the ingredients plenty of faith. Then mix well and spread over a period of a lifetime. Serve to everyone you meet!

Delane Stevens, President
2013-2014 Service League of Cherokee County

YOUR FAVORITE RECIPES

Recipe   Page Number

INDEX OF RECIPES

Meats & Main Dishes

Vegetables

Breads, Rolls & Pastries

Cakes, Cookies & Desserts

Beverages, Microwave & Miscellaneous

INDEX OF RECIPES **E**

LIST OF CONTRIBUTORS

ORDER FORM

For additional copies of this fine cookbook, please complete and mail the order form to:

Service League of Cherokee County
P.O. Box 1132
Canton, GA 30169

- -

Please mail me _____ copies of your Cookbook at $14.95 per copy plus $5.95 for shipping and handling per book. Enclosed is my check or money order for $_____ .

Mail books to:

Name _____

Address _____

City _____ State _____ Zip _____

- -

Please mail me _____ copies of your Cookbook at $14.95 per copy plus $5.95 for shipping and handling per book. Enclosed is my check or money order for $_____ .

Mail books to:

Name _____

Address _____

City _____ State _____ Zip _____

Publish Your Own Cookbook!

Hometown Recipes Raising Funds for You!

...ding recipes has been a popular hobby for ...erations. Now you can turn this tradition into ...xciting and profitable fundraising program that ...lves your entire community!

...dcraft helps you every step of the way with a proven ...raising plan that guarantees your success!

...uest your FREE copy of our Recipe for Success ...ishing Guide that explains how easy it is to publish ... own cookbook for fun and profit!

Recipe for Success
1 Very Low Price— 67 Days to Pay!
No Money Down!
Delivery Within 60 Working Days!

Raise $500 to $25,000 with our ...aranteed Cookbook Fundraising Program

H4-14

...der Your Free Recipe for Success Publishing Guide Today!

"...u Collect
...Recipes...
...dcraft will
...the rest!"

Organization_____

Name _____

Address_____

City_____ State_____ Zip _____

Home Phone_____

Email _____

www.fundcraft.com • info@fundcraft.com

We Have Your Recipes for Successful Fundraising

Cookbooks are proven fundraisers and perfect keepsakes. Preserve treasured recipes from your church, school, family or organization. We make it affordable, profitable and fun!

Creating your own unique cookbook with hometown recipes is an easy, enjoyable way for groups of all sizes to raise money. All over America, churches, schools and groups like yours are earning thousands of dollars selling their personalized cookbooks using the proven Fundcraft Cookbook Program.

Return the postage paid card today or visit us online fundcraft.com.
100% Made in the U.S.A.

COOKING
HINTS & TIPS

• Keep a recipe card upright by placing it in the tines of a fork and putting the fork handle in a glass.

• To keep a recipe book or card clean, place it under an upside-down glass pie plate. The curved bottom also magnifies the print.

• Use a photo album as a recipe book. Each time you cut a recipe out of a magazine, place it in one of the album's plastic sleeves.

• Glue an envelope to the inside of the front cover of your 'favorite' cookbook to hold new recipe cards or recipe clippings.

• Before you start baking or cooking, keep a plastic bag handy to slip over your hand when the phone rings.

• If butter is used in place of vegetable shortening, the amount of butter should be at least 1/4 more than the amount of shortening.

• It is best to cream butter by itself before adding the sugar.

• When a chocolate cake requires greasing and flouring the pans, try using cocoa instead of flour. When the cake is done, there will be no white flour residue on your cake and it adds flavor.

• Before measuring honey or other sticky ingredients, dip your spoon in oil.

• Put cold oil in a hot pan so the food won't stick.

• Add a pinch of baking soda to your frosting and the frosting will stay moist and prevent cracking.

• When you boil water, place a lid on the pot and the water will come to a boil in a shorter period of time– saving at least 10 minutes.

• To keep dough from sticking to your rolling pin, cover it with a clean stockinette.

• For shiny pie crusts, brush the crust lightly with milk.

• For sugary pie crusts, moisten the crust lightly with water or beaten egg whites, then sprinkle with sugar.

• Never salt food to be fried– it will draw moisture to the surface and cause spattering in the hot oil.

• Before heating the fat when deep fat frying, add one tablespoon white vinegar to minimize the amount of fat absorbed by the frying food. The food will taste less greasy.

• Sugar can be powdered by pounding it in a large mortar or rolling it on a paste-board with a rolling pin. It should be made very fine and always sifted.

COOKING HINTS & TIPS

• No more slow cooker mess—Before you start the recipe, place a turkey size browning bag in your cooker and put the ingredients inside the bag. After serving your dinner, just take the bag out and throw it away.

• Here's a neat casserole trick: When you are baking a covered casserole, keep your dish and oven neat by propping the lid open just a bit with a toothpick. This will prevent the casserole from bubbling over.

• Use double-thick paper towels to place over cooling rack to keep the rack from making imprints into the cake while cooling.

• Use one 3" pan instead of 2" layer pans for a higher cake—more cake less work. Slice lengthwise for layers.

• To make any home-made or boxed chocolate cake recipe moist and fluffier, add a spoonful of vinegar to the dry ingredients. You'll be amazed at the difference.

• Dip your icing spatula in hot water and dry with a paper towel. The heat from the water will melt the oil in the icing making it smoother.

• When you need a cake cooled and out of the pan quickly, place a cold wet towel or paper towels under the pan.

• Out of icing for your cup cakes? Just pop a marshmallow on top of each cup cake for about a minute before they come out of the oven. It will make a delicious, instant gooey frosting.

• Use dental floss to cut cakes, especially delicate, sticky ones that tend to adhere to a knife.

• Extend the shelf life of your home-made or store-bought cakes, by storing a half apple with them.

• Store a few lumps of sugar with your cheese to prevent it from molding.

• Applesauce is a great fat substitute for low fat baking. Simply substitute half the fat in a recipe with an equal measure of applesauce.

• Disinfect your kitchen sponges by placing them in the microwave for 60 seconds.

• Peeled apples, pears and potatoes in cold, slightly salted water, helps keep them from turning brown.

• If soup tastes very salty, a raw piece of potato placed in the pot will absorb the salt.

• You can cut a meringue pie cleanly by coating both sides of a knife lightly with butter.

COOKING & FOOD TERMS

AL DENTÉ– Describes foods, especially pasta, cooked only until soft enough to eat, but not overdone. The Italian translation is "to the teeth."

BLANCH– Blanching is a process in which food is briefly plunged in boiling water for a moment, then immediately transferred to ice water to stop the cooking process. Blanching tomatoes or peaches for about 20 seconds makes them easier to peel.

BROIL– To cook food directly under or over heat source, usually in the oven under the top broiling element or on the grill.

EGG WASH– Egg yolk or white mixed with a small amount of water or liquid then brushed over baked goods to give color and sheen.

JIGGER– A liquid measure equal to 1-1/2 fluid ounces.

JULIENNE– To cut food into thin, matchstick strips. Julienne strips are usually about 1/8 inch thick, but the length varies.

KNEAD– A technique used to mix and work dough, usually using the hands. Dough is pressed with the heels of the hands, while stretching it out, then folded over itself.

MARINATE– To let food soak in a seasoned liquid in order to flavor and tenderize.

MINCE– To chop food into small pieces, usually 1/8 inch or less.

PARE– To cut the skin from a food, usually with a short knife called a paring knife.

PUREE– To blend, process, sieve, or mash a food until it's very smooth and has the consistency of baby food.

ROAST– To cook food in an open pan in the oven, with no added liquid.

SAUTÉ– To cook quickly in a pan on top of the stove until the food is browned.

SIMMER– To cook liquid at about 185° or just below boil. Tiny bubbles just beginning to break the surface.

THICKEN– To make liquid more thick by reducing or adding a roux, cornstarch, flour or eggs.

WHIP– To beat ingredients with a whisk, or other utensil, which incorporates air into a mixture and changes the texture.

INGREDIENT SUBSTITUTIONS

INGREDIENT	AMOUNT	SUBSTITUTE
Baking Powder	1 tsp.	• 1/3 tsp. baking soda and 1/2 tsp. cream of tartar • 1/4 tsp. baking soda and 1/2 cup sour milk or buttermilk (Decrease liquid called for in recipe by 1/2 cup.)
Bread	1 slice dry 1 slice soft	• 1/3 cup dry bread crumbs • 3/4 cup bread crumbs
Broth, Beef or Chicken	1 cup	• 1 bouillon cube dissolved in 1 cup boiling water • 1 envelope powdered broth base dissolved in 1 cup boiling water • 1 1/2 tsp. powdered broth base dissolved in 1 cup boiling water
Butter	1 cup	• 7/8 to 1 cup hydrogenated fat and 1/2 tsp. salt • 7/8 cup lard plus 1/2 tsp. salt • 1 cup margarine
Buttermilk (sour milk)	1 cup	• 1 cup plain yogurt • 1 cup whole or skim milk plus 1 Tbsp. lemon juice or white vinegar • 1 cup milk plus 1 3/4 tsp. cream of tartar
Chives, Finely Chopped	2 tsp.	• 2 tsp. green onion tops finely chopped
Chocolate, Chips Semisweet	1 oz.	• 1 oz. sweet cooking chocolate
Chocolate, Semisweet	1 2/3 oz. 6 oz. pkg.	• 1 oz. unsweetened chocolate plus 4 tsp. sugar • 1 cup
Chocolate, Unsweetened	1 oz. sq.	• 3 Tbsp. cocoa plus 1 Tbsp. fat

INGREDIENT SUBSTITUTIONS

INGREDIENT	AMOUNT	SUBSTITUTE
Cream, Light (18% to 20% fat)	1 cup	• 3/4 cup milk and 3 Tbsp. butter or margarine (for use in cooking or baking) • 1 cup evaporated milk, undiluted
Cream, Whipped	2 tsp.	• Chill a 13 oz-can of evaporated milk until ice crystals form. Add 1 tsp. lemon juice. Whip until stiff
Dates	1 lb.	• 2 1/2 cups pitted
Dill Plant, Fresh or Dried	3 heads	• 1 Tbsp. dill seed
Egg, Whole, Uncooked	1 large (3 Tbsp.)	• 3 Tbsp. and 1 tsp. thawed frozen egg • 2 1/2 Tbsp. sifted, dry whole egg powder and 2 1/2 Tbsp. lukewarm water • 2 yolks 1 Tbsp. water (in cookies) • 2 yolks (in custard, cream fillings, and similar mixture) • 2 whites as a thickening agent
Eggs, Uncooked	1 cup = ▸	• 5 large • 6 medium
Egg White	1 large (2 Tbsp.)	• 2 Tbsp. sifted, dry egg white powder, and 2 Tbsp. lukewarm water
	1 cup = ▸	• 8 large egg whites
Egg Yolk (1 1/2 Tbsp.)	1 yolk	• 3 1/2 Tbsp. thawed frozen egg yolk • 2 Tbsp. sifted, dry egg yolk
	1 cup = ▸	• 12 large egg yolks
Fines Herbes	1/3 cup	• 3 Tbsp. parsley flakes, 2 tsp. dried chervil, 2 tsp. dried chives, 1 tsp. dried tarragon

INGREDIENT SUBSTITUTIONS

INGREDIENT	AMOUNT	SUBSTITUTE
Flour, All-purpose (for thickening)	1 Tbsp.	• 1 1/2 tsp. cornstarch, arrowroot starch, potato starch, or rice starch • 1 tsp. waxy rice flour • 1 1/2 Tbsp. whole wheat flour • 1 tsp. quick-cooking tapioca
Flour, All-purpose	1 cup sifted	• 1 cup and 2 Tbsp. cake flour • 1 cup rolled oats, crushed
	1 lb.	• 4 cups sifted • 3 1/3 cups unsifted
Flour, Cake	1 lb.	• 4 3/4 cups
	1 cup sifted	• 1 cup minus 2 Tbsp. sifted all-purpose flour
Flour, Self-rising	1 cup	• 1 cup minus 2 tsp. all-purpose flour, 1 1/2 tsp. baking powder, and 1/2 tsp. salt

NOTE: Substitutes for white flours added to most baked goods will result in a reduced volume and a heavier product. Substitute no more than 1/4 of white flour in a cake to ensure success. In other recipes, you can substitute whole wheat flour for 1/4 to 1/2 white flour.

Garlic	1 clove	• 1/8 tsp. garlic powder
Gelatin, Flavored	3 oz.	• 1 Tbsp. plain gelatin and 2 cups of fruit juice
Honey	1 cup	• 1 1/4 cups sugar and 1/4 cup water
Ketchup	1 cup	• 1 cup tomato sauce, 1/4 cup brown sugar, and 2 Tbsp. vinegar (for use in cooking)
Lemon Juice	1 tsp.	• 1/2 tsp. vinegar
Lemon Peel, Dried	1 tsp.	• 1 to 2 tsp. grated fresh lemon peel • 1/2 tsp. lemon extract

INGREDIENT SUBSTITUTIONS

INGREDIENT	AMOUNT	SUBSTITUTE
Marshmallows, Miniature	1 cup	• 8-10 regular
Mayonnaise	1 cup	• 1/2 cup yogurt and 1/2 cup mayonnaise • 1 cup of sour cream
Milk, Buttermilk	1 cup	• 1 cup sweet milk and 1 3/4 tsp. cream of tartar
Milk, Skim	1 cup	• 1/2 cup evaporated milk and 1/2 cup water
Milk, Sweetened	1 can (about 1 1/3 cups)	• Heat the following ingredients until sugar and butter are dissolved: 1/3 cup plus 2 tsp. evaporated milk, 1 cup sugar, and 3 Tbsp. butter or margarine
Milk, Whole	1 cup	• 1 cup reconstituted non-fat dry milk (Add 2 Tbsp. butter or margarine, if desired.) • 1/2 cup evaporated milk and 1/2 cup water
Mustard, Dry	1 tsp.	• 1 Tbsp. prepared mustard
Onion, Fresh	1 small	• Rehydrate 1 Tbsp. instant minced onion
Onion, Powdered	1 Tbsp.	• 1 medium onion • 4 Tbsp. fresh chopped
Onion	1 lb.	• 3 large onions • 2 to 2 1/2 cups chopped
Orange Peel, Dried	1 Tbsp.	• 2 to 3 Tbsp. grated orange peel
Parsley, Dried	1 tsp.	• 3 tsp. fresh parsley, chopped

INGREDIENT SUBSTITUTIONS

INGREDIENT	AMOUNT	SUBSTITUTE
Pumpkin Pie Spice	1 tsp.	• 1/2 tsp. cinnamon, 1/4 tsp. ginger, 1/8 tsp. allspice, and 1/8 tsp. nutmeg
Shortening, Melted	1 cup	• 1 cup cooking oil (Substitute only if recipe calls for melted shortening)
Shortening, Solid (used in baking)	1 cup	• 1 1/8 cups butter (Decrease salt called for in recipe by 1/2 tsp.)
Sour Cream, Cultured	1 cup	• 1 cup plain yogurt • 3/4 cup milk, 3/4 tsp. lemon juice, and 1/3 cup butter or margarine
Sugar, Brown	1 cup firmly packed 1 lb. = ▶	• 1 cup granulated sugar • 2 1/4 cups firmly packed
Sugar, Granulated	1 lb. = ▶	• 2 1/4 cups
Sugar, Powdered	1 lb. = ▶	• 3 3/4 cups
Sugar, Granulated	1 tsp.	• 1/8 tsp. noncaloric sweetener solution or follow manufacturer's directions
Sugar, Granulated	1 cup	• 1 1/2 cups corn syrup (Decrease liquid called for in recipe by 1/4 cup.) • 1 cup of powdered sugar • 1 cup, brown sugar, firmly packed • 3/4 cup honey (Decrease liquid called for in recipe by 1/4 cup; for each cup of honey in baked goods, add 1/2 tsp. soda.)
Tomato Juice	1 cup	• 1 cup tomato sauce and 1/2 cup water
Yogurt, Plain	1 cup	• 1 cup of buttermilk • 1 cup of sour cream

HERBS & SPICES

ALLSPICE– Usually used in ground form, allspice has a flavor like a combination of cinnamon, nutmeg, and cloves. Allspice is used in both savory and sweet dishes.

BASIL– Most people are accustomed to using fresh basil in their favorite Italian dishes, but this licorice-like herb is equally at home in Thai coconut curry or a Provencal pistou. Dried basil tastes completely different from fresh, so if you want to add a shot of basil flavor try blending basil with olive oil and storing cubes in the freezer.

BAY LEAF– A pungent flavor. Available as whole leaf. Good in vegetable and fish soups, tomato sauces and juice. Remove before serving.

CARAWAY– Their slightly anise flavor works particularly well with rye breads as well as with the kind of sweet and sour dishes favored in Central Europe such as pork and apples or braised red cabbage.

CARDAMOM– Whole cardamom pods can appear in pilaf rice, curries, or Scandinavian baked goods. Ground cardamom loses its flavor.

CAYENNE PEPPER– A touch of spicy cayenne can add a lot of heat to a dish without radically changing the flavor. It is a mixture of ground chili peppers and can be used in a wide variety of cuisines.

CELERY SEED– The wild celery plant seeds are on more and more menus emphasizing regional and local cuisine. The seeds add their pungent flavor to anything from cocktails to coleslaw and can be used whole or ground.

CHIVES– Leaves are used in many ways. May be used in salads, cream cheese, sandwiches, omelets, soups, and fish dishes.

CILANTRO– This herb is truly a love it or hate it proposition. Stems are quite sweet and can be added raw along with the leaves while the roots are prized by Thai chefs for curry pastes.

CLOVE– Often paired with cinnamon and nutmeg, cloves are dried flower buds that are sold both ground and whole. They have a warm, sweet flavor that works great with sweet and savory, like clove studded ham. For a more potent flavor grind them yourself.

CUMIN– Can be experienced in all kinds of dishes from Mexico, India and the Middle East. The toasted seeds can be used whole in dishes and eaten as is, or be ground right before use. Pre-ground cumin loses potency quickly, but can be helped by toasting first in a dry skillet over medium-low heat.

DILL– The feathery leaves of the dill plant add light anise flavor to seafood, soups, salads, and lots of other dishes. Dill is almost always added at the very last minute. Keep fresh in the refrigerator by storing it in a glass of water with a plastic bag placed over the top.

MUSTARD– Mustard is great to have around to add heat and a piquant flavor in sauces, dressings, marinades, and entrees. Whole mustard seeds are often part of the pickling spices, but are also a key part of many Indian curries where they are toasted in oil first until they pop.

NUTMEG– An aromatic spice with a sweet and spicy flavor. Nutmeg adds warmth and depth to foods but doesn't overpower other ingredients.

HERBS & SPICES

OREGANO– A pungent herb primarily found in Mediterranean and Mexican cuisines, it is one of the few herbs that survives the drying process relatively unscathed. Use dried oregano for longer stewing or dry rubs, but make sure to use half as much dry as you would fresh since the flavor is so intense. Oregano can also be used as a substitute for its close cousin marjoram.

PAPRIKA– Paprika has too often been relegated to the role of garnish, mostly because of its beautiful rich color. There are all sorts of paprika that can add flavors from mild to hot.

PARSLEY– Formerly regulated to the role of garnish, fresh parsley is coming into its own for its fresh flavor and great health benefits, but dried parsley lacks both flavor and color.

RED PEPPER– Dried red chili pepper sold either ground or in flakes, red pepper works well either added early to dishes that are going to cook for a while or simply shaken on near the very end. Because they vary greatly in terms of heat, taste your red pepper to see just how hot it is.

ROSEMARY– Can be used fresh or dried for long cooking in soups, meats, stews and more. Use sparingly at first and more if needed.

SAGE– Used fresh. May be used in poultry and meat stuffings; in sausage and practically all meat combinations; in cheese and vegetable combinations, or curry.

TARRAGON– Experimenting with this anise-like herb in classic French favorites such as bearnaise sauce, creamy tarragon chicken, or fresh vinaigrette can help you learn how to use tarragon to lift flavors without overpowering a dish.

THYME– One of the most popular herbs in American and European cooking, thyme can be paired with nearly any kind of meat, poultry, fish, or vegetable. To use fresh thyme, peel off as many of the leaves as you can from the woody stem by running your fingers along the stem.

VANILLA– An aromatic spice with a warm flavor, vanilla is the seed pod of an orchid. It's available dried or as an extract.

FRESH SEASONINGS

- In recipes, cut salt in half and add more fresh herbs and spices.
- When doubling a recipe, herbs and spices should only be increased by one and a half times. Taste, and then add some if necessary.
- Add sage, bay leaf and garlic at the beginning of the cooking process as they have a strong flavor. Herbs with more subtle aroma such as basil, parsley, fennel are best when added at the end of the cooking process to preserve their flavor.
- Delicate aromas can be lost due to overcooking.
- Cut or chop fresh herbs to expose more surface area. This will release more flavor.
- Here's a chart to convert dried herbs to fresh

1 tsp. dried herbs	=	1 Tbsp. fresh herbs
1/8 tsp. garlic powder	=	1 medium clove of garlic
1 tsp. onion powder	=	1 medium onion, finely chopped
1 tsp. ground ginger	=	1 tsp. grated fresh ginger

THE
FOOD PLATE

Follow the *__Food Plate__* below so you can enjoy a more balanced meal. Cooking healthy is an easier way to help you eat smart!

Set goals. Cook healthy. Eat smart.

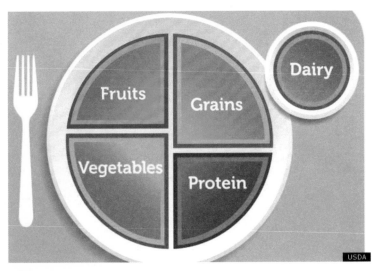

*USDA Approved Food Plate

COUNTING CALORIES

CANDIES, SNACKS & NUTS

Almonds	12 to 15	93
Cashews	6 to 8	88
Chocolate Bar (nut)	2 ounce bar	340
Coconut (shredded)	1 cup	344
English Toffee	1 piece	25
Fudge	1 ounce	115
Mints	5 very small	50
Peanuts (salted)	1 ounce	190
Peanuts (roasted)	1 cup	800
Pecans	6	104
Popcorn (plain)	1 cup	54
Potato Chips	10 medium chips	115
Pretzels	10 small sticks	35
Walnuts	8 to 10	100

DAIRY PRODUCTS

American Cheese	1 cube 1 1/4 inch	100
Butter, margarine	1 level Tbsp.	100
Cheese (blue, cheddar, cream, Swiss)	1 ounce	105
Cottage Cheese (uncreamed)	1 ounce	25
Cream (light)	1 Tbsp.	30
Egg White	1	15
Egg Yolk	1	61
Eggs (boiled or poached)	2	160
Eggs (scrambled)	2	220
Eggs (fried)	1 medium	110
Yogurt (flavored)	4 ounces	60

DESSERTS

Cakes:

Angel Food Cake	2" piece	110
Cheesecake	2" piece	200
Chocolate Cake (iced)	2" piece	445
Fruit Cake	2" piece	115
Pound Cake	1 ounce piece	140
Sponge Cake	2" piece	120
Shortcake (with fruit)	1 avg. slice	300
Cupcake (iced)	1	185
Cupcake (plain)	1	145

Pudding:

Bread Pudding	1/2 cup	150
Flavored Pudding	1/2 cup	140

Pies:

Apple	1 piece	331
Blueberry	1 piece	290
Cherry	1 piece	355
Custard	1 piece	280

Lemon Meringue	1 piece	305
Peach	1 piece	280
Pumpkin	1 piece	265
Rhubarb	1 piece	265
Ice Cream:		
Chocolate Ice Cream	1/2 cup	200
Vanilla Ice Cream	1/2 cup	150
Miscellaneous:		
Chocolate Eclair (custard)	1 small	250
Cookies (assorted)	1, 3-inch dia.	120
Cream Puff	1	296
Jello, all flavors	1/2 cup	78

BREADS & FLOUR FOODS

Baking Powder Biscuits	1 large or 2 small	129
Bran Muffin	1 medium	106
Corn Bread	1 small square	130
Dumpling	1 medium	70
Enriched White Bread	1 slice	60
French Bread	1 small slice	54
French Toast	1 slice	135
Macaroni and Cheese	1 cup	475
Melba Toast	1 slice	25
Noodles (cooked)	1 cup	200
Pancakes, wheat	1, 4-inch	60
Raisin Bread	1 slice	80
Rye Bread	1 slice	71
Saltines	1	17
Soda Crackers	1	23
Waffles	1	216
Whole Wheat Bread	1 slice	55

BREAKFAST CEREALS

Corn Flakes	1 cup	96
Cream of Wheat	1 cup	120
Oatmeal	1 cup	148
Rice Flakes	1 cup	105
Shredded Wheat	1 biscuit	100
Sugar Krisps	3/4 cup	110

FISH

Bass	4 ounces	105
Brook Trout	4 ounces	130
Crabmeat (canned)	3 ounces	85
Fish Sticks	5 sticks or 4 ounces	200
Haddock (canned)	1 fillet	158
Haddock (broiled)	4 ounces (steak)	207

COUNTING CALORIES

FRUITS

Apple (raw)	1 small	70
Banana	1 medium	85
Blueberries (frozen/unsweetened)	1/2 cup	45
Cantaloupe Melon	1/2 melon large	60
Cherries, fresh/whole	1/2 cup	40
Cranberries (sauce)	1 cup	54
Grapes	1 cup	65
Dates	3 or 4	95
Grapefruit (unsweetened)	1/2	55
Orange	1 medium	70
Peach (fresh)	1	35
Plums	2	50
Tangerine (fresh)	1	40
Watermelon	1" slice	60

MEATS

Bacon (crisp)	2 slices	95
Frankfurter	1	155
Hamburger (avg. fat/broiled)	3 ounces	245
Hamburger (lean/broiled)	3 ounces	185
Ham (broiled/lean)	3 ounces	200
Ham (baked)	1 slice	100
Lamb Leg Roast	3 ounces	235
Lamb Chop (rib)	3 ounces	300
Liver (fried)	3 1/2 ounces	210
Meat Loaf	1 slice	100
Pork Chop (medium)	3 ounces	340
Pork Sausage	3 ounces	405
Roasts (beef)		
Loin Roast	3 1/2 ounces	340
Pot Roast (round)	3 1/2 ounces	200
Rib Roast	3 1/2 ounces	260
Rump Roast	3 1/2 ounces	340
Spareribs	1 piece, 3 ribs	123
Swiss Steak	3 1/2 ounces	300
Veal Chop (medium)	3 ounces	185
Veal Roast	3 ounces	230

SALADS & DRESSINGS

Chef Salad/mayonnaise	1 Tbsp.	125
Chef Salad/French, Roquefort	1 Tbsp.	105
Cole Slaw (no dressing)	1/2 cup	102
Fruit Gelatin	1 square	139
Potato Salad (no dressing)	1/2 cup	184
French Dressing	1 Tbsp.	60
Mayonnaise	1 Tbsp.	110

NAPKIN FOLDING

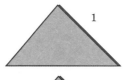

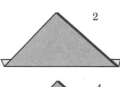

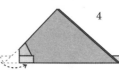

CANDLE

Candle Fold Instructions:
1. Fold into triangle, point at top.
2. Turn lower edge up about 1".
3. Turn over, folded edge down.
4. Roll tightly from left to right.
5. Tuck in corner. Stand upright.

DIAGONAL STRIPE

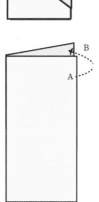

Diagonal Stripe Fold Instructions:
1. Fold edge A to edge B.
2. Fold edge A to edge B. Loose edges at top.
3. Roll down the top flap.
4. Roll down the second flap
5. Roll down the third flap
6. Fold sides back as pictured.

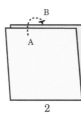

TABLE SETTINGS

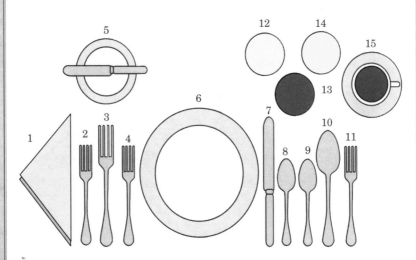

FORMAL TABLE SETTING

1. Napkin
2. Salad fork
3. Dinner fork
4. Dessert fork
5. Bread-and-butter plate, with spreader
6. Dinner plate
7. Dinner knife
8. Teaspoon
9. Teaspoon
10. Soup spoon
11. Cocktail fork
12. Water glass
13. Red-wine glass
14. White-wine glass
15. Coffee cup and saucer

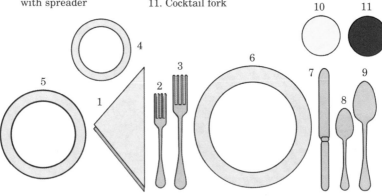

GENERAL TABLE SETTING

1. Napkin
2. Salad fork
3. Dinner fork
4. Bread-and-butter plate
5. Salad plate
6. Dinner plate
7. Dinner knife
8. Teaspoon
9. Soup spoon
10. Water glass
11. Wine glass

- **Don't put out utensils that won't ever be used.**
- **Bring the coffee cup and saucer to the table with the dessert.**